LONDON TRANSPORT RAILWAY SIGNALLING

PAPERS ON THE LIFE AND WORK OF ROBERT DELL 1900-1992
Signal Engineer to the London Passenger Transport Board and its successors

CONTENTS:

Page 3: Preface.

Page 4: Robert Dell - An Introduction, by Eric Eden, MBE, FIRSE.

Page 8: Robert Dell's Life and Work in a National Context, by John Talbot.

Page 22: Robert Dell's Development of the Automatic Driving System for the Victoria Line, by Keith Ware, BSc, C Eng, FIEE, FIMechE.

Page 36: Robert Dell's Patents, by John Tilly, MIRSE, FPWI, MCIT, FRSA.

Page 49: written contribution from Ronald J. Post, OBE, C Eng, MIEE, MIRSE.

Page 52: Bibliography.

Page 56: Extended captions to the cover photographs.

Published by: **NEBULOUS BOOKS**
Cromwell House, 11 Oliver Rise, Alton, Hampshire, GU34 2BN
Tel: 01420 89264
ISBN 0 9507416 5 5
Copyright: © The individual authors/**NEBULOUS BOOKS** 1999.
Typesetting and page layouts by Nebulous Books, Alton.
Printed by The Amadeus Press Ltd, Huddersfield.

THE LIFE AND WORK OF ROBERT DELL

Above: Robert Dell, one of several LT official staff portraits; this one, undated, was taken by Walter Bird. *Photo: London Transport Museum (WM.5253-F)*

THE LIFE AND WORK OF ROBERT DELL

PREFACE

In 1995, Dr Michael Duffy created a series of seminars from the School of Engineering & Advanced Technology at Sunderland University. The school was also the Centre for Engineering Change, and is now the School of Computing, Engineering and Technology. Other sponsors were the Newcomen Society, and the London Transport Museum (particularly Mark Dennison) who provided the venue on 2 March 1996 for a meeting on the work of Robert Dell.

After a personal introduction by Anthony Bull, CBE, OBE, (Vice-Chairman of the London Transport Board from 1965 to 1971) formal papers were read by four authors. The audience then visited Cobourg Street (London Underground's control room for the Northern and Victoria Lines) to see Dell's equipment there.

A further author, Ronald Post, responded afterwards, and the sponsors kindly agreed to all the papers being collated and published. Since they are not being reported as proceedings or transactions in the true sense, opportunities have been taken, with the authors' consent, to enhance the information they contain. For convenience, a single bibliography has been included at the end, in addition to which some further references and remarks are made as footnotes.

Sadly, Eric Eden, who warmly supported this work, died on 13 August 1998.

It is hoped that the resulting book, now available to a much wider audience than those present at the seminar, will be a fitting tribute to a man whose influence on the safe daily travelling of so many of London's commuters, has been profound. The full implications of the major changes to signalling which were introduced by Robert Dell during his career, are adequately reflected in the illustrations on the front and back covers of this book. These reflect the scene at the beginning and the end of his long career on London Transport's railways. A fuller explanation of this surprising contrast is given as a page of extended captions to the three cover photographs, which will be found together on page 56.

Publisher's acknowledgements:
The publisher would like to thank Sheila Taylor of the London Transport Museum, Mike Horne and Joel Kosminsky for their help with this publication. Ronald Post helped with tracking down various elusive bibliographical references, obtaining details of Dell's membership of the various professional institutions and kindly read the text through at various stages. But the greatest thanks must be due to John Talbot for acting as co-ordinating editor - a task which undoubtedly speeded up the completion of this long awaited publication!

THE LIFE AND WORK OF ROBERT DELL

ROBERT DELL - AN INTRODUCTION

by Eric Eden

Eric Eden (1926-1998) died before the publication of this book. He retired in 1992, his post then being Safety Engineer for Signalling and Control Systems for London Underground. He then continued working, mainly to create a National Licensing System for signal engineering staff. He also travelled to the National Railway Museum at York to assist with the preparation of a monograph on signalling, and he actively encouraged many other projects. His other interests included a love of opera.

I first heard of Mr Dell when I started as an office boy in the Signal Engineer's Office at Earls Court in April 1941. I did not actually see him until some time later when I was allowed to enter his office and place some documents in his 'in' tray. In those days everybody in any position was a 'Mr' and it was Mr Dell throughout his career. Even at his retirement at the age of seventy, he was always Mr Dell to all his colleagues and staff. This was the custom in those days. In all my career with him I never heard anybody ever call him Robert. I note with interest that Keith Ware, who is a contemporary of mine, automatically calls his paper 'Dell's', whilst the younger authors use Robert. Whilst we are on names, Robert Dell's nick name was 'ding-dong'. This was used by most of his staff without intending any disrespect. I worked for Mr Dell until he retired in 1970, a period of 29 years.

Robert Dell was born in Childs Hill, London, NW2 on 25 February 1900, the son of a landscape gardener. Although in his early years he was brought up surrounded by the plants and flowers of his father's business, his interests quickly showed themselves in electrical and mechanical things. He felt a need to know how things worked and he was already constructing equipment before he reached his teens.

It was natural therefore for him to embark on a technical career and after elementary school, he joined the Underground Group as an apprentice in February 1916, in the Signal Engineer's Department. His apprenticeship lasted until July 1920, during which time he undertook a variety of duties including: machine and instrument shop work; installation and maintenance of automatic signal apparatus; drawing office work; a period of training in the machine shop of the Permanent Way Department. He also served in the First World War, but only in this country. His technical education was obtained from the then Regent Street Polytechnic and included Electrical Engineering and Mechanical Engineering. He also studied English, Chemistry, Physics and Mechanics on the general education side.

After completing his apprenticeship in July 1920, he became Junior Technical Assistant in the Signal Engineer's Department. He was soon given section responsibilities in the drawing office. In December 1922, he became in overall charge of 'New Works' on signalling throughout the Underground system, his title changing to New Works Assistant, Signal Department. He was responsible for carrying out the installation of signalling on the extensions to Hendon and Morden on what would later become the Northern Line. In January 1925, he became Outdoor Assistant to Signal Engineer, Underground Railways, responsible for all signal work, both installation and maintenance. After the formation of the London Passenger Transport Board in July 1933, he was appointed Assistant Signal Engineer in October that year. He became an Officer in February 1936, by which time his duties included the maintenance of automatic ticket machines and the design of special apparatus. By the end of 1937, the Signal Engineer's Department included: Signal Installation staff (5 supervisors and 250 men); Machine & Instrument Shop, plus the maintenance of 8 petrol lorries (2 supervisors and 60 men); Maintenance of Automatic Ticket Issuing Machines (1 supervisor and 30 men), as well as management and Drawing

THE LIFE AND WORK OF ROBERT DELL

Office staff. He made innovative ideas and many design patents were registered in his name. Many of these were items which would ensure the fail safe operation of the Underground system. This he was successful in achieving and his record during his time with London Transport was exemplary.

Soon after becoming an Officer in 1936, he was asked to go to New York as part of a team, 'to investigate and report upon the maximum capacity of train service which is being operated on the New York Subways, with a view to determining the maximum capacity of train service which it would be possible to operate upon the Board's system of railways'. The other members of the team were Messrs. J.P. Thomas (General Manager, Railways), Evan Evans (General Superintendent, Railways), and W.P.N. Edwards (Secretary to the Chairman), and the visit lasted from 26 May to 11 June 1936. This report, ***Report on Maximum Capacity of Train Services - New York and London***, included examining the building of express relief lines as one method of increasing the capacity of existing underground lines - notably on the Central and Northern Lines. (It was this report which later influenced the eventual siting of the deep-level tube shelters built by the LPTB as agents of the Ministry of Home Security in 1941-42. Lengths of twin tunnels of a diameter which suited initial use as air-raid shelters were built at eight locations, sited on the lines proposed in the report. This was with the idea that they could be linked up after the war, and reflected Ashfield's clever strategy to get some of these lines built without direct cost to the LPTB!)

Dell was appointed Joint Signal Engineer at the age of forty in 1940 and at the end of 1941, after I joined the department, he was promoted to Signal Engineer responsible for the whole department. This was a very difficult time for the London Underground as the war was on with the London Blitz in full swing. It meant keeping it running notwithstanding firstly the bombs and then later the V1s and V2s, and at the same time carrying millions of passengers in safety. He also organised and ran a wartime factory in the passenger subway between Earls Court Station and Earls Court Exhibition building, which made bombsights for the Royal Air Force. Some of the work was carried out in the Signal Overhaul Shop at Lillie Bridge. When I started my apprenticeship in 1943, my first job was to bend copper tube all day, which was needed for part of the bombsight. Another idea Robert developed was equipment to detect unexploded bombs. This was required if they fell in the vicinity of the Underground tunnels that ran under the River Thames. This knowledge was necessary as floodgates were closed in the tunnels during air-raids and opened after the all-clear was sounded, unless an unexploded bomb was detected. The ultimate goal of automatic[1] floodgates was eventually achieved. The signals were naturally interlocked with the floodgates in a fail safe manner.

A further development by Robert Dell enabled the working of lever frames by means of compressed air cylinders. This system permitted remote control from a distant cabin. From the 1930s there were several major changes[2] in these methods of route-setting and remote-control. John Talbot and John Tilly will highlight the main ones: North Acton in 1947 and Farringdon in 1954 (later followed by Programme Machine working which led to the present systems at Cobourg Street). Dell's paper on this topic, entitled 'Power Worked Lever Remote Control Signalling System' was published in the proceedings of the Institution of Railway Signal Engineers for 1942.

After the war he continued to make safety his priority, developing increased train frequency and timetable reliability. Telephones, closed circuit television and automatic fare collection were also part of his responsibilities. However the development and creation of the new Victoria Line system soon became his main involvement. Throughout the 1950s and 1960s, he concentrated on a completely

---
[1] Unlike automations such as British Railways' half-barrier level crossings, all LT floodgates have been protected by signals (with train-stops). The hydraulic gates, numbers 31-50 (the final two being on the Victoria Line), were capable of being switched to centrally-monitored operation.

[2] There were also over twenty minor variations in the equipment; in fact few of the similar cabins were technically identical.

THE LIFE AND WORK OF ROBERT DELL

automatic railway line with driverless trains running over track that was equipped with such sophisticated signal control systems, that a service could be provided to passengers that would be the safest and most efficient ever achieved. Indeed, when the Victoria Line opened in 1968-69, it was an example to rapid transport systems throughout the world. In the 1958 New Year's Honours List, he was awarded the OBE and attended an Investiture at Buckingham Palace on 18 February 1958. In 1965 he was awarded the George Stephenson Prize and Medal by the Institution of Mechanical Engineers.

He retired at the age of seventy, having completed the Victoria Line system and having started the expansion of the automatic fare collection system, which he planned to cover the entire London Underground. He had therefore served London Transport and the Signal Engineer's Department for fifty-four years. After retiring, he was asked to advise on the Caracas, Venezuela Railway and he visited Tokyo and New York. He was also retained as a consultant in 1971 to advise on the Melbourne Underground.

The following is a list of papers produced by his staff that appeared in **IRSE Proceedings** during the latter half of his career, which indicates his range of work (a list of Dell's own papers will be found on page 52):

Date:	Author:	Title:
1947	H.W. Firminger	Signalling Installation Work on the London Transport System
1949	W. Owen	Speed Control Signalling for Close Headway Working
1950	H.W. Hadaway	Improvements in Track Circuit Shunts (Injector Track Circuits)
1950	P.W. Ottley	London Transport Communications
1952	W. Owen	Special Signalling for Temporary Speed Restrictions (London Tube Lines)
1960	W. Woodhouse	Putney Line Programme Machines
1960	H.W. Hadaway	LTE Methods for the Control and Locking of Junctions
1964/65	G.R. Kent & H. Duckitt	Development of Automatic Train Operation on LT
1966/67	R. Ravenscroft	Line Production Overhaul of Signalling Equipment
1966/67	V.H. Smith	Victoria Line Signalling Principles
1966/67	B.F. Sharp	Automatic Fare Collection on LT Railways
1966/67	H.W. Hadaway	Fail Safe
1967/68	E.W. Wager	LT Railway Control Rooms
1969/70	F.G. Maxwell	Victoria Line in Operation *

* This last paper, by London Transport's Operating Manager (Railways), records Robert Dell's success on the Victoria Line project.

THE LIFE AND WORK OF ROBERT DELL

Robert Dell died on 10 October 1992. When he was born, the railway constituents of the LPTB had about 100 surface or free-standing sub-surface signal cabins and 60 deep-level cabins in tube rooms. When he died, these were reduced to 20 and 4 of each type, with the addition of four control centres (Cobourg Street, Earls Court, and two at Baker Street). During the same period Westinghouse supplied 5,094 levers in 204 new frames.

My remarks so far relate to my knowledge of Robert Dell as one of his staff. I have been fortunate to recently have a discussion with someone who was Robert's boss during the latter part of his career with London Transport and is therefore able to comment from a different viewpoint.

This was Anthony Bull, former Vice Chairman of the LTB and Board Member for Railways and Staff. He told me that whilst Robert specialised in Railway Signalling, he was able to discuss and suggest ideas in many other areas, such was his widespread knowledge of engineering. Anthony Bull chaired weekly meetings with the Chief Officers of all the various engineering disciplines employed on the Underground, where he was able to form this opinion.

Anthony Bull also recalled that on the day when the Queen opened the Victoria Line, the responsible Director of the Westinghouse Company, which manufactured the equipment at Chippenham, told him that Dell had persuaded Westinghouse to manufacture equipment which they had thought to be impossible!

ROBERT DELL'S MEMBERSHIP OF PROFESSIONAL INSTITUTIONS (each of which kindly supplied information from their files):

The Institution of Mechanical Engineers
Associate Member from 1937
Member from 1944 (Members were re-designated as Fellows in September 1967)

The Institution of Electrical Engineers
Student from 1921
Associate Member from 1928
Member from 1944 (Members were re-designated as Fellows in 1966)

The Institution of Railway Signal Engineers
Student from 1921
Associate Member from 1925
Member from 1928 (Members were re-designated as Fellows in November 1969)
Honorary Fellow from 1969

> Robert Dell was elected to the IRSE Council in 1938. In 1945, he became Chairman of the organising Committee, which position he retained until 1948. He was elected Vice President in 1947 and President for the year 1949. He was elected President again for a second year in 1966, a rare achievement.

*Note: A photograph of Robert Dell will be found on page 4 of **IRSE Proceedings** for 1949. A photograph of Robert Dell, with Col. D McMullen and Anthony Bull (both mentioned in the text) will be found on page 25 of **IRSE Proceedings** for 1966/67. A further photograph of Robert Dell will be found on page 189 of **Underground Railways of the World**, by O.S. Nock (Adam & Charles Black) 1973.*

THE LIFE AND WORK OF ROBERT DELL

ROBERT DELL'S LIFE AND WORK IN A NATIONAL CONTEXT

by John Talbot

John Talbot is a member of the Signalling Record Society and has been their Corresponding Member for London Transport for over ten years. He earlier learned the practical art of signalling as a Territorial Army Officer with access to the Longmoor Military Railway. He later joined Her Majesty's Prison Service, in 1971, and served in Yorkshire, Winchester, Northern Ireland, Worcestershire, London (three times), the Isle of Wight, Surrey and Oxfordshire. These postings allowed him to see a good proportion of UK signalling. His other interests include a passionate one in the Ashington Colliery area of Northumberland. Since 1995 he has held a non-academic post in Oxford University's Museum of the History of Science.

INTRODUCTION

My qualification to present this paper is entirely one of chance. Since the 1950s I have visited well over a thousand signal boxes in England, including all in London, and studied the available documents on UK signalling, including much relating to Robert Dell. In 1989 I was the last Governor of the now closed Oxford Prison and I dined with the Oxfordshire County Councillors. Next to me was the late Cllr David Calvin-Thomas of Wallingford, and he inquired if I had any particular hobby. Using an occasional impish sense of humour I said I studied the interlocking of points and signals on the Underground. David Calvin-Thomas simply replied that he would introduce me to his neighbour Robert Dell. And so it happened that I paid several visits to Robert Dell at his Wallingford, Oxfordshire home where he still treasured a retirement present - a model Programme Machine made by the Acton apprentices. We corresponded between my visits. He was very kind to me. I think he was amazed that an interest should be shown by someone with a job so unrelated to the railway industry, and I think he liked an impish sense of humour, and he liked David Calvin-Thomas' devotion to caring and the community which by chance had brought us together. Robert Dell knew I would later share my knowledge with others and I think he would be very happy for many of his exact words to be presented here, together with some of my own research results. I still treasure a hand written letter from him answering about twenty of my questions, and he concluded that he thought I knew more about the history of his signalling than he did! But he was a very modern man, rather than a romantic historian.

Bob Bird, who deals with signalling for the London Transport Museum, says he discovers Robert Dell to have been a very private person. Perhaps I was the privileged recipient of Dell's disclosures. Eric Eden reminded us of the convenience that Dell's ages equalled the calendar years, and that formalities have given rise to different names, varying between Sir and Robert. I would have preferred to use both of those words - but will have to settle for the Oxfordshire name Robert Dell.

DELL'S EARLY YEARS

Robert Dell joined the Metropolitan District Railway in 1916. We shall call it, as it often was called, 'the District', and this is helpful because differences with the Metropolitan Railway will be significant. He won a prize for best apprentice, and particularly remembered joining Mr Cornish (the power frame fitter), on Saturday nights to remove and clean the mechanical interlocking between the miniature levers of the power frames. Both the interlocking[3] and the frames were originally exports from America. Whitechapel (see front cover photographs) is the only one of those distinctive cabin buildings remaining

---

[3] It was patented in the USA (No.406212 of 2 July 1889) by James T Hambay, and known as 'Hambay's cross-locking'.

now, and those cabins and their first frames dated from reframing of the important busy places and outdoor resignalling with the electrification of the District, from 1905. Later on, Robert Dell had to speak sharply to architects to preserve the extra height of cabin roofs, shown by the extra upper window panes (below the street wall) at Whitechapel, to maintain an ambient temperature for the frames, a rudimentary air-conditioning. This design feature was carried on elsewhere, for example at Manchester (Victoria West, Irwell Bridge Sidings and Deal Street cabins) in 1929.

District reframing went on into the less busy areas, well illustrated at Ealing Common in 1925, where the full size Saxby & Farmer frame (see figure 1) was replaced by a style B miniature frame from Westinghouse Brake and Saxby Signal Company (see figure 2). Several features of Robert Dell's apprenticeship and learning-period arise, and we can now compare his professional development with that of present-day signal engineers. The new frame is not in the manufacturer's list, either before or after their 1920 factory move from Kings Cross to Chippenham. This tells us that the District began the conservation of frames by moving them, or sections of them, from cabin to cabin. Saving capital costs became important. Both photographs show illuminated diagrams and 'rotary' Train Describers, key parts of the District's 'integrated' systems. Note also, the standard practice of giving the signalman only the few track-circuit indications approaching his cabin which he actually needs: This became contrary to later national practice, and is still found on some lines operated by London Underground Limited. Signalmen's needs will emerge again as Robert Dell acted on or re-acted to them. The District's 'integration' was largely not found elsewhere in the world. The Drum, Ribbon, or Magazine Describers, and their successors, have had a long life, modernised versions still being installed in 1963 (in East Putney cabin for working to Earls Court). John Tilly's paper will refer to the patent. They provided customer service with platform indications about the approaching trains, as do the 1990s dot matrix indicators. A cabin amalgamation scheme appears: a purpose of this re-framing is to abolish, three

Figure 1: Ealing Common signal box interior on 23 February 1925, before the old frame was replaced. *Photo: London Transport Museum (U3391)*

Figure 2: Ealing Common signal box interior on 10 March 1925, just after the new lever frame was installed. Details of all the equipment are given in the text. *Photo: London Transport Museum (U3478)*

months later, the next cabin westwards (Hanger Lane Junction) and put its area on the vacant end of the diagram and its control onto spare miniature levers, just visible beyond the signalman in the photograph above. Saving wages became important.

It is worth considering exactly where Robert Dell was in the development of all power-signalling. Remote control of signals applying through points at great distances from cabins is so common today that it disguises the fact that it did not begin in that way. At the turn of the century, and for about the next quarter century, there was no power operation of points at distances greater than those of mechanical working from cabins. Excepting the Liverpool Overhead, only the District, parts of the Metropolitan, a little of the London & South Western Railway on the surface, and the tubes (with their important early signals of spectacles without arms), had any 'integrations' between power signalled station yards, long plain sections, and track circuits. Elsewhere, as at Glasgow, Hull and Newcastle, contemporary power signalling was in reality no more than power transmission for quicker working of points, without cumbersome mechanical ground detection, and the old block instrument system (or even exemptions from it) was retained. The District system was Electro-Pneumatic (EP), a misnomer as it fails to mention the mechanical interlocking in the frames, on which Robert Dell trained.

THE DIFFERENCE WITH THE METROPOLITAN

The most modern of the Metropolitan Railway's signalling systems then, were Electro-Mechanical and All Electric, both misnomers too, but the important difference between the two partly sub-surface London railways was that air, controlled by low voltage valves, powered the District points, and electricity directly powered the Metropolitan points. The latter had not been the first application as motors on Currie's principle had been trialled at Gloucester in the 1880s and installed in the reversing sidings

THE LIFE AND WORK OF ROBERT DELL

east of Earls Court in the 1890s. They failed to be successful then, principally because of the lack of men able to maintain them. Low voltage remote versions began at Potling No.2 Junction near Ashington in Northumberland towards the end of the first quarter of the 20th Century but were so slow in operating, about 20 seconds, they were abandoned as a British standard sometime after 1934. The Metropolitan trains would never have left Baker Street if three points needed a minute to operate, with primary batteries on a large scale, so high voltage was used by the Metropolitan. The difference between the two railways really annoyed Robert Dell. He felt the Metropolitan's signal engineers failed to innovate[4] (they were led by Major Rupert Falshaw Morkill - a scion, ironically, of my own family). John Francis' book[5] does reveal they duly changed minds to suit Robert Dell's. The unheralded difference between the systems was that EP was virtually fire-proof, and the travelling public's debt to Robert Dell is the greater for that, sadly in the circumstances of non-signalling fires since. Of course there have been detractors, who hurt Robert Dell, saying the EP was cumbersome, but they did not experience the alternative risks.

CAREER DEVELOPMENT

Having described the railway signalling scene Robert Dell entered, we very nearly lose him after 1918. Again mercifully for the travelling public's future safety, his war service was in England, and on demobilisation all he could get was a job planing point blades at the District's Lillie Bridge Mechanical Engineering Shop. William Stephen Every was then newly appointed Signal Engineer, and by chance the pair met on the Earls Court platform going home one evening. As they talked, Every recalled Robert Dell's prize-winning apprenticeship and on the strength of that memory immediately offered him a job in the Earls Court Signal Drawing Office. The stage was set, and history begun, by that chance meeting and Every's selective mind. We can still stand under the same train-shed roof at Earls Court and think of that occasion. Robert Dell's offices looked out onto the west end of the station. Much later, at least one prototype device was installed on the trackside there so he could see it operating from his window.

At Earls Court then, Mr Proud was the chief draughtsman, his brother being at Westinghouse (the frame suppliers), and Robert Dell and Mr Leaney did signalling circuits. The only other staff in the drawing office was just one man to do the signs (station signs were dealt with by the Signal Engineer's Department), a remarkable contrast with later staffing levels, considering the District's position in the vanguard of progress.

In 1924 Robert Dell became Every's Chief Assistant, and in 1932 he had completed his own main task, of resignalling the South Harrow line. 'When the Metropolitan came in', as Robert Dell described it, the companies' amalgamation was more about settling old scores and some very interesting developments occurred. The Metropolitan's electric points were failing in wet weather but more significantly some signalling circuitry there was on high pole routes. These were allowed to remain for telephones only, and EP introduced. Robert Dell felt the Metropolitan had been full of discipline rather than thinking, contracting-out instead of getting contractors to meet one's wishes. Every and Dell, who clearly had a good 'governor & deputy' relationship, did not reject 'all-electric' working without it having been given an apparently fair trial on their Underground Group's 1924 new surface line to

---

[4] It could be said the Metropolitan was in-step and was innovative with its 1932 Stanmore signalling. However, this was a bought-in (rather than Dell-style negotiated) American Centralised Traffic Control (CTC) system, which allowed for no increase in traffic and was really only suitable for long rural railways, using Field Station (FS) relay rooms. It proved to be unwanted in England (and hence the Stanmore maintenance costs to the LPTB rose). Only one other branch (the Isle of Sheppey with four FSs in 1959) was commissioned, and CTC schemes for branches in East Yorkshire and at Llandrindod Wells for the Central Wales Line were actually aborted.

[5] *The Style 'L' Power Frame*, by J.D. Francis (published by the author), 1989, ISBN 0 9514636 0 8.

THE LIFE AND WORK OF ROBERT DELL

Edgware, where it economised against the cumbersome components of EP (particularly the compressed air main). Similar circumstances were forced on the LPTB for the signalling at Stanmore for many years.

In his paper, Keith Ware will mention Robert Dell's attitude to committee work, and I particularly remember his ability to sort out who was best at what, and to entirely reject committee government or cabinet collective responsibility, except of course when government or cabinet decisions were his alone.

Looking at the Northern Line again, so many attempts were made to improve the service, including for instance lengthening trains, that it is not surprising it features in this paper. Robert Dell was very scathing about J.P. Thomas' committee scheme for non-stop looping at Brent, saying it was a matter of chance if at most less than a minute was saved, and he, Robert Dell, did not in the final analysis leave things to chance! All this must have made for very lively committee or inter-departmental meetings, and now a welcome new development for historians is Peter Bancroft's listing of official papers relating to London Transport held at the Public Record Office (Part One was published in 1996), though I doubt this will console the losers in what must have been very personalised office disputes. The Signal Department was the strongest and most prestigious within LT.

LOCAL ROUTE SETTING

In the 1930s there was a clear divergence between the LPTB and the others, the main-line railways, about new signalling. Led by the North Eastern Area of the LNER, the provincials (encouraged by their own cabin amalgamation schemes) went for switch panels with electrical circuitry which did not differentiate between near and distant sites. Control panels and relay interlocking were in their cabins in the 1930s, 40s and 50s, with enormous relays, and no facility for automation. W.S. Every retained lever frames for his new schemes of control but quickly went to route setting at a number of sites. Each was technically different, but at all sites some points followed by signals could be changed after one manipulation of a lever or switch [6]:

Wood Green - 1932 (This included Britain's first pure relay-interlocking)
West Kensington area - 1934
Rayners Lane & South Harrow Gas Works - 1935
Cromwell Road area - 1936
Finchley Road area - 1937
Elephant & Castle - 1941 (see figure 3)

(A scheme for Lambeth North was not proceeded with)

A year into the Second World War when Robert Dell was 40 and Morkill was 65 (as was Every who died that year), Mr Robertson, their chief, told Morkill to retire. But he knew Pringle who got him a Government job and work on Her Majesty's Railway Inspectorate (H.M.R.I.). (He is remembered for his courteous, kindly and dignified bearing.) The stage is now re-set for further progress by Robert Dell alone. The Drawing Office staff then was much larger compared with 1916, an increase from four to seventy-eight.

---

[6] Contemporary illustrated details of most of these installations are within the bibliography. Rayners Lane was born out of adversity - runaway ballast wagons shattered the previous cabin on 22 November 1934. A cabin with switches is shown in figure 21.

THE LIFE AND WORK OF ROBERT DELL

FUTURE DEVELOPMENT

Relationships with H.M.R.I. have always been important. Colonel Sir John Pringle, Chief Inspector, introduced national revised requirements for railway signalling in 1925 with some spoken comments which span everything in this paper:

'I feel impelled to refer to what I regard as the pre-eminently satisfactory conditions which obtain on electrically operated Underground and Tube railways, due to the methods of track circuiting, signalling and automatic control which have been universally adopted. Far less risk is attendant upon journeys by such lines than is nowadays the case in passenger transport upon roads, whether with horse-drawn or motor-driven vehicles. The companies operating these lines deserve the highest credit for attaining so conspicuous a standard. I recollect, twenty years ago (1905), when I was first intimately concerned with the new signalling system on the electrification of the District Railway, being warned by a distinguished predecessor in office, since deceased, of the danger of approving such systems. He expressed his surprise that I was able to sleep at night with so great a responsibility on my shoulders. It is true that I have lost no hard-earned rest by accepting the responsibility. But the incident taught me a lesson, which I shall never forget, that it is most necessary to keep an open mind upon all new methods of railway operation, signalling or construction, and not to regard conservatism in relation to past practice as a necessary virtue. I commend the maxim to the attention of railway friends'.[7]

Much of this, the responsibility, the achievements, the winning of modernisation over conservatism, became Robert Dell's successes. He remembered a much later encounter with the Inspectorate when the Aldwych branch was being considered for automatic operation without drivers. I regret I did not ask him whether two trains were considered. I think the idea at that early stage was to have no staff member on board at all, because H.M.R.I.'s response was to suggest staff with nothing else to do would wait at platform ends to run into the tunnel and detrain the passengers, if necessary. Unfortunately this finished that scheme, and practical Automatic Train Operation (ATO) development went next to the surface, as Keith Ware's paper will tell us. H.M.R.I. were surprisingly pro-active. Robert Dell considered automation of every line on the underground map, with early schemes for the South Acton and East London Lines and an Aldwych branch extension to Waterloo. Col. D. McMullen, one of Col. Sir John's successors (who had recommended approval of ATO for public use in April 1963), said British Railways should have it, first on the Waterloo & City, next on the London, Tilbury & Southend. Commuters would have been well served had these men got their way! Major Peter Olver, retiring from the Inspectorate, was asked by me in the early 1990s what he remembered of Robert Dell and LT. With the Olympian candour so typical of the great Inspectorate he stated 'Robert Dell and LT were doing supremely well what they had always done - safeguarding the travelling public'.

Robert Dell, as the other papers say, was keen on all kinds of developments, large and small. He particularly remembered the introduction of two-way loudspeakers for communication with trainmen. These were actively discussed as early as 1932 for the new Northfields Depot, together with controlled points and track-circuiting[8] to reduce accidents and the need for shunters (coming out of sidings being the pinch point of starting the service). The depot yards were another area where the LPTB and main-line railways diverged, over signalling. The latter concentrated on improvements to their large-scale freight yards (such as Feltham, Wath, Banbury and March) with hardly anything being done about stabling passenger carriages. The LPTB were almost alone in improving siding working for empty passenger trains, and this has now resulted in the present set of depot control panel towers at Upminster (1958), Northumberland Park (1967, panel replaced 1989), Stonebridge Park (1979) and Neasden

---

[7] He was speaking at the Institute of Transport Congress in London, 13-16 May, reported in ***Railway Engineer***, July 1925, page 229.
[8] None of these were in fact installed there then.

THE LIFE AND WORK OF ROBERT DELL

Figure 3: The limited space in a tube tunnel room at Elephant & Castle (the Bakerloo Line's 1941-91 cabin) on 30 December 1987. The frame was style N, mainly for push-pull route setting. *Photo: John Talbot*

(1988, with the first computer-based interlocking). As befits areas without loaded passenger trains, the signalling provision can be different, together with radio supplanting the loudspeakers. At South Harrow Depot land used for exercising dogs was outside the railway fence. The loudspeakers were so sensitive they could detect even a grunt from a dog. The signalman could turn them up and respond with a 'woof-woof' to cause consternation! Dell was proud of having got contractor suppliers to meet his demands, and for lever frames the specification was a model of overview combined with detail and stern instructions concluding with great persuasive force, 'Only best materials to be used in manufacture and first class workmanship required throughout... complete details of the design shall be submitted to the Signal Engineer and the design shall meet with his approval in every respect'. This was the Westinghouse style N frame (from 1931), exclusive to LT, still interlocked largely in accordance with the old District's turn-of-the-Century import from America. Legend has it that the first 'Mind the gap' recorded announcement (at Bank, Central Line) was Robert Dell's own voice. This would have been typical of him! I have the tape, but regret not asking him who did it, and when.

Dell was undoubtedly a task-master and he did what many leaders do, talk with the workers on the ground. It has been said elsewhere, and he confirmed it to me, that the idea of programme machines came from a face to face argument with a signalman at Camden Town. He had visited the new push-button room at Ealing Broadway and told Robert Dell he wouldn't work them in his cabin. On the other hand there are still small antiquities on LT railways, and Robert Dell's sense of financial economy made him remember the exact origins of the surviving ground frames at Golders Green, Morden (which he personally bought second-hand in the 1920s for the opening of the line), and Totteridge, all now working to Cobourg Street.

THE LIFE AND WORK OF ROBERT DELL

FIFTY YEARS OF DEVELOPMENT AND PROGRESS OF THE SIGNALLING OF LONDON TRANSPORT

This was the title of a lecture for Robert Dell to give, dated 8 October 1969. He felt the development of signalling of the underground railways could be divided into three phases:

1) The first phase really occurred more than fifty years earlier and comprised the original installation of power signalling, and in 1919 the installation was roughly fifteen years old.

2) Phase two covered thirty years from 1919 to 1949 and comprised a period of detailed improvements, standardisation, increased safety and improved reliability, without great changes in the actual principle of the signalling.

3) Phase three covers the twenty years from 1949 to 1969 and could be described as 'into automation'.

Giving all the details would make this paper too long, but the equipment of each phase was:

PHASE 1:
1.1   Semaphore signals in open, moving spectacles in tunnels
1.2   Train Stops
1.3   Power Frames
1.4   Safety Circuits

PHASE 2:
2.1   The D.C. Track Circuit
2.2   Early A.C. Track Circuits
2.3   Thermal Regulators
2.4   The two-element Vane Relay
2.5   The Condenser Feed track circuit
2.6   Train Stop proving
2.7   Point ground lock
2.8   Redesign of the Two Element Vane Relay (culminating in the highly successful detachable tops)
2.9   Daylight colour signals
2.10   Fire Proofing
2.11   Segregation of cables
2.12   Redesign of equipment
2.13   Power frame improvement
2.14   Signalling cable improvement
2.15   Signalling cable insulation
2.16   Circuitry improvement
2.17   Standardisation of signal aspects
2.18   Remote control
2.19   Push button desks
2.20   Improved headway signalling
2.21   Speed control signalling

THE LIFE AND WORK OF ROBERT DELL

This enormous list of detailed improvements, increasing safety and reliability, being carried out whilst nurturing the organisation along to later automation, almost defies any one man to hold everything in mind. Additionally a great number of signal cabins were changed over to new equipment by being temporarily replaced (see figure 21 for an example), and when those temporary installations went wrong, if they did, it must have caused the exclamation that being attacked by an alligator makes you forget your journey is actually to get across the swamp.

The question has been asked, why the D.C. Track Circuit (TC) is in Phase 2, when it has been a main component of Phase 1. TC lengths differ and the locations of their electrical feeds, returns, and relays can be chosen. By 1922 Robert Dell had discovered that despite all the 1905 precautions by the American exporter Harold Gilbert 'Buster' Brown (from Melrose, Massachusetts), stray traction current *could* cause a wrong-side TC failure, negating all the safety systems. It might be momentary, and confined to a longer train only when the centre of that train coincided with the centre of a longer TC which was mid-way between traction substations. Dell told Every of this risk. The long-term solution was to convert all TCs to those in Phase 2.5. As this process took 29 years to complete it belongs to Phase 2. It could be said Dell anticipated fragmentation of railway management, for example train lengths, signalling, and sub-stations being decided independently without an overview of the consequences. One of the older TC relays (from cabin EN, see photograph on the front cover) is exhibited in the LT Museum. This relay is called famous for its longevity in service, not for the secret fault in its system.

Robert Dell was particularly specific to me about item 2.10 Fire Proofing. On 4 August 1935 a plane crashed near Colindale cabin. Debris linked traction current and signalling circuits and the resultant fire disabled the cabin beyond repair. Robert Dell attended the site and automatic through-running was put in within 24 hours. Outside cabling was diverted to a new large temporary wooden hut and a spare power frame ex-stores[9] brought into use in there within a week. Prior to this, policy was not averse to wood for cabin structures, doors and door frames, window frames, roofs, relay shelves, power frame cabinets, nor averse to lead for cable covering, and fire proofing was limited to resistance for 5 minutes to a dropped cigarette. Immediately after the fire Robert Dell changed policy to brick, metal, concrete and tiling for cabin structures and to steel and aluminium shelving, Craig Park fireproof wiring and metal power frame cabinets inside cabins. Morden was the first cabin to be altered to meet the new policy and most others subsequently were.

PHASE 3:
- 3.1 The Programme Machine
- 3.2 Parsons Green
- 3.3 Electronic circuits
- 3.4 Automatic Train Operation
- 3.5 Twin relays
- 3.6 Signal supervision and traffic control

For the only time, one place-name appears. Parsons Green was arguably the most difficult depot (see figure 4), with eleven sidings distributed at both ends of the station on both sides of the running-lines, and some sidings were entered or left by making a 'shunt-back' along another. Coupling and un-coupling to shorten or lengthen trains was also a feature. When it was planned to remotely control the site from Earls Court, the staff for there announced indignantly they had 'never done hand coupling'.

---

[9] 'Signal Cabin in a garden', **Pennyfare**, November 1935, pages 459-460, gives other details, and states that the frame came from the signalling school.

THE LIFE AND WORK OF ROBERT DELL

So Robert Dell devised a Local Siding Allocation Panel, with remnant magnetic relays, so that the Parsons Green supervisor could dial in to the Programme Machines to effect small temporary service changes.[10]

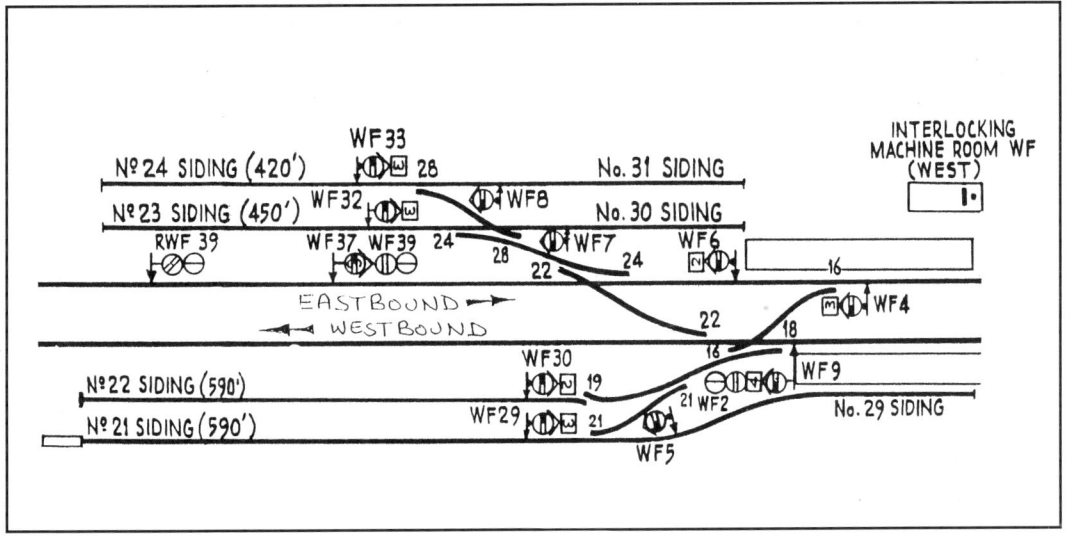

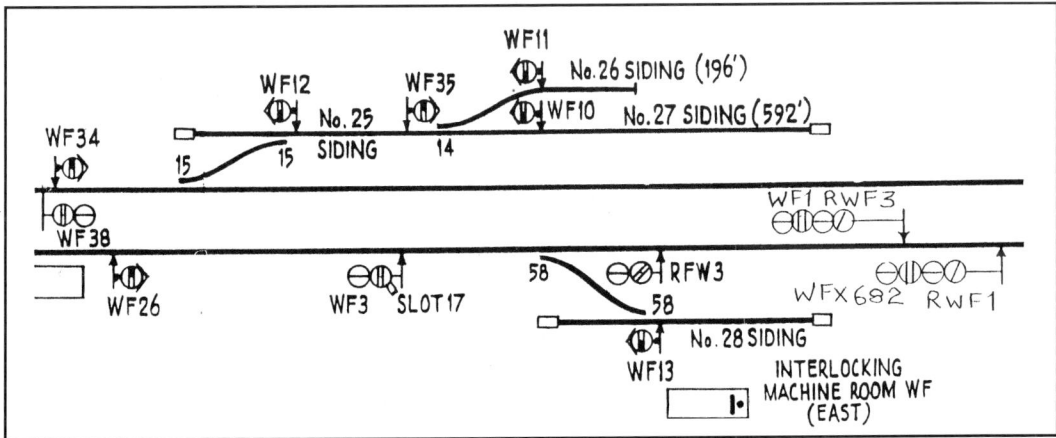

Figure 4: Parsons Green Depot layout from 15 November 1963. This drawing also shows the way LT numbered their sidings in a separate series from their platforms (unlike BR!). Nos. 26 and 30 have since been removed.
Diagram: London Underground Limited

References to such Trade Union negotiations are appropriate. A long time ago I asked Sid Weighell, when we were both on a train in our native Yorkshire Wensleydale, about this. He was the National Union of Railwaymen's HQ officer responsible for LT matters from 1961 (before ultimately becoming General Secretary). He liked the 'first class attitude' of LT's top men. He thought the staff didn't appreciate the sort of management they had. Negotiations with LTE included the Departmental Head instead of facing a British Railways type Personnel Department. Robert Dell he regarded as a top class man, widely sought after as a problem solver.

---
[10] Described and illustrated in ***Trains Illustrated*** for December 1960, pages 756-758.

THE LIFE AND WORK OF ROBERT DELL

TOWARDS CENTRALISED CONTROL

Power Frames were part of the District inheritance and Robert Dell pressed contractors to provide what he wanted. The 1938 specification was updated. Now fitted with air motors, and, as a matter of important detail, the lever catch handles removed, these local frames (styled N2) could be remotely controlled by intervening post-office type wiring and relay-interlocking. An importance of this development is that it belies the legend that LPTB lines were solely mechanically interlocked (additionally there was always at least one pure relay installation): It allows remote control by less expensive wiring and relays (Light Secondary Conductors), with the result that any electrical interference between the control place and the remote frame, where heavily armoured cables (Primary Conductors) commence, would simply result in the local locking jamming before any signal cleared. In the normal course of events the commands via relay-interlocking make no 'mistakes' to cause mechanical jamming. In any failure a signalman takes back local hand-control, just by turning off the air.[11]

Despite many published claims, including that in the **Railway Gazette**, about North Acton being the first, it was in fact at Shoreditch in 1943 that an air-worked frame was first used, the subject of an illustration (see figure 15) and patent in John Tilly's paper. Robert Dell himself said that North Acton was the first, but what he meant was that it was the first air-worked frame down-the-line from a controller (the Wood Lane, later White City signalman) who exercised route-setting. Shoreditch was lever-for-lever replication down-the-line from Whitechapel East London cabin. Even so, North Acton in 1947 was over a decade in advance of Main-Line practice, as British Railways first had any comparable equivalent only after the 1955 British Transport Commission Modernisation Plan adopted the 50 cycle system of electrification. Traction current then caused new signalling just as on the District fifty years earlier. To give BR security against irregular functioning, induced voltage and other adverse effects, they first remotely controlled relay rooms, by carrier and transitionised equipment operating on the scanning principle over a minimum of wires, in 1958. That was at Styal, Heald Green, East Didsbury and Mauldeth Road between Crewe and Manchester.

ROUTE DETERFLEX SIGNALLING SYSTEM

This system is so significant, so unlike British Railways practice, and so little publicised, that it should be recorded here in detail. W.H. Challis (shown in figure 17) wrote the specification dated 10 November 1937, nearly a decade before the equipment was in use. There were twelve sketches of the following features:

1. As there are no point levers at the controlling cabin, points and crossovers are given three figure numbers for reference.

2. The manned controlling cabin has push-pull three-position route levers, each controlling two routes. There are two operating wires per pair of routes between the controlling cabin and the interlocking. Flexibility of operation permits a signalman to move his levers for a second and possibly conflicting route before the first train has cleared a preceding route. At the controlled interlocking an emergency locking frame with two-position full-stroke levers is provided for operation of signals and points. All controlling and interlocking relays are located here.

3. When a route lever is normally mid-way d.c. is put on the line wire. When in the push or pull position (which chooses the route) a.c. is put (on the operating wire for that route) to feed the switching of signal and point circuits at the controlled interlocking.

---
[11] There are other tasks, and staff to be present or consulted, but the simplicity is important.

THE LIFE AND WORK OF ROBERT DELL

4. Point control relays.

5. Ground locks.

6. Point indication.

Numbers 4-9 are the less unusual parts of the system

7. Signal control.

8. Route checking relays.

9. Signal lock relays and lever lock circuits.

10 & 11. Control lever lock circuits between the two cabins together with the slot (LT terminology) relay wiring for automatic working.

12. The method of repeating track circuit signal and point indications back to the controlling cabin by means of d.c. with telephone type relays and cable.

I apologise that such a brief description does not do justice to this system; but sketch 2 mentioned above is really at the very heart of this remarkable signalling system, with its aim of 'Rapid Restoration in case of any failure'.

FRAME CHANGE
In the 1950s when it was clear there would be no further frames for working by signalmen, the 'table' construction on which the locking was between the front legs, the electric contacts between the back legs, the electric locks along the top of the table, and the levers on the front edge of the 'table', was entirely abandoned in favour of the table being straightened-out vertically.[12] Mechanical interlocking is now at the bottom, electric contacts at the top, and emergency handles between them, all on rotating shafts. Effectively the 'kitchen-table' frame becomes an 'Upright Piano', style V, of which an example is in the London Transport Museum. Robert Dell claimed to be the designer of this, though that is open to question and interpretation of the patent (mentioned in John Tilly's paper).

W.S. Every had earlier famously remarked, 'God knows what it costs to dig a hole in the underground?' He was referring to both starting the job and carting away the excavated material within the tube's brief nightly absence of trains. The developing specifications included swift maintenance to the frame by access from a depth below it, so (despite appearances we have already seen) table frames had been really suitable only for elevated (two-storey) cabins on the surface, rather than for cabins which were rooms in tube stations. The frame change really was about 'saving space'.

PUSH BUTTONS AND PROGRAMME MACHINES
The controls were initially push-buttons, again products of Robert Dell's pressure on contractors. Later there were local unmanned programme machines[13], in which, briefly, the timetable ran on a punched roll and feelers detected what had to be signalled and then did so. The local Signalman gave way to centralised Regulators, so called because they supervised and intervened only when things were out of the usual course. For that, they had elements of push-buttons. The push-button controls were first installed at Ealing Broadway in 1952 in a dedicated desk supplied by Westinghouse. Some of

---
[12] Illustrated in John Tilly's paper (see figure 16).
[13] Further details and an illustration are in John Tilly's paper (see figure 17 and illustration on back cover).

Figure 5: The interior of Amersham signal cabin on 4 April 1988, showing push-button controls in a larger desk. The left hand group controls Amersham area, the right hand group Chalfont and the Chesham branch. The suppliers (Westinghouse) 'W' badge is on the desk end in the foreground. *Photo: John Talbot*

these desks, like frames, were conserved and moved around from site to site. The most recent example of this event was the desk from Wembley Park (1954-1987) being moved into Farringdon signal cabin in 1987, ready to control the Aldgate triangle from 1988. Of course the individual buttons were altered to suit, but the desk and type of apparatus remained the same; it was just like re-configuring a lever frame and its interlocking for moving from cabin to cabin. At Amersham (see figure 5), and a few other cabins, there were larger desks or pairs of desks so one or two signalmen could control more extensive areas. At Farringdon in 1955, for the first installation via the new style V frame mentioned earlier, the buttons for Aldersgate were wall mounted, probably because the first train movement could be signalled and a second immediately pre-selected (to be automatically initiated when the first had cleared). This had been done since 1952 elsewhere. The time the signalmen had to spend at the buttons was very little, freeing him for his local duties.

Additionally, by 1956 further pre-selection of remote route-setting turned back locomotive-hauled trains at Liverpool Street (Metropolitan & Circle Lines bay platform) and Moorgate (widened lines two BR terminal platforms) including completely 'stepping-back' the locomotives by attaching one from spurs. After the train had made its reversed departure, the original arrival-locomotive was signalled back into the spur ready for the next complete occasion, all done sequentially by one pre-selection, without the remote signalman's constant attention. This was inarguably Britain's most complex

THE LIFE AND WORK OF ROBERT DELL

advanced signalling installation, and I think it has only been matched since by BR's present automatic route setting. It was dispensed with, only because locomotives were. Button controls were subsequently also frame mounted as at Rickmansworth, again for an existing local cabin to additionally control a distinctly separate area or areas.

At Cobourg Street (see figure 6) the Northern Line apparatus, of Diagram, Describer and Control Buttons, is fitted (for all-line control) in the order of Describer (at the top), with Programme Machine repeating indications between Describer and Diagram, and buttons in one desk for about five regulators or senior signalmen (a saving of 24 compared with the earlier local cabins). Programme machine rolls for other days of different services are held ready to be taken to local site, the whole of the Northern Line being controlled from here (excepting Morden shunters area which has been previously mentioned, but for which the space seen at the right hand end was provided).

In the same room is another long desk, for one or two regulators, for the whole of the Victoria Line (again excepting its depot), and both desks are overseen from the rear by line controllers (Supervisors, not Signalmen) who in turn are overlooked by an Information Officer who completes feedback to the public.

My account is up to date in 1990, since when smallish detailed alterations have been planned for some of the equipment I have described. Elsewhere a new generation of signalling has already started, on the Central Line, and everything we are discussing today will ultimately be history.

The future regimes, of 'risk assessment' and 'safety cases', may entail public visits to signal boxes being rarely granted. I gratefully acknowledge all the help I have been given by railway staff.

Figure 6: The Northern Line apparatus at Cobourg Street control room on 21 July 1987, further details of which are given above. *Photo: John Talbot*

THE LIFE AND WORK OF ROBERT DELL

ROBERT DELL'S DEVELOPMENT OF THE AUTOMATIC DRIVING SYSTEM FOR THE VICTORIA LINE

by Keith Ware

Keith Ware started his working life with the LMS Railway on a two year post graduate course at St. Rollox Works, Glasgow. He moved to London Transport in 1950, working on train performance, brake testing, tunnel gauging, etc. In the 1960s he became involved in automatic driving developments and hence in the trainborne use of electronics - not the only steam man to move into this field, but one of a rather select band. He was given the title of Electronics Engineer in 1965, but then became involved in management, first as Deputy Design Engineer for LT Buses and Trains, and then in charge of Train Design and development at the time the Central Line rolling stock was being initiated. His last job with London Transport was as Client Engineer on the Docklands Light Railway, following which he has done consultancy work in Canada, Hong Kong, Cairo, Wakefield and Folkestone.

BACKGROUND

The history of mass transit is a patchwork of technical and organisational changes interspersed with periods of consolidation. Bringing in major changes to a large, satisfactorily running system sets major problems, but pressure is always there to reduce costs and increase safety and comfort. Robert Dell during his long career developed principles and techniques which allowed him to make many major advances with relatively little trouble.

The introduction of programme machine control of local interlockings allowed signalling manpower to be reduced (as noted elsewhere).

Some features of his approach were:

1. The separation of safety functions from others.

2. Keeping the Safety element as simple as possible, using carefully designed and proven components, and in particular using mechanical devices where possible for the most vulnerable elements.

3. Decentralisation of control so that the service can be kept running even if the main control room is put out of action.

4. Taking advantage of modern techniques, particularly electronics, for the non-safety elements. In this he was prepared to be in the forefront of the use of advanced technology, although cautious in his selection of circuitry and components.

Bearing in mind the industrial use of electronics was in its infancy in the late 1950s Dell's adoption, for example of multiplexing for remote control, was very bold. In contrast his use of mechanical interlocking between points and signals was quite conservative.

Dell was clear that the future of mass transit railways in developed countries depended on increasing automation of all functions where this was appropriate. Having facilitated reductions in signalling staff, and at the same time providing vastly improved control and information, he turned his thoughts to the trains. There was a precedent for automation allowing a reduction in train crews

- when automatic doors were introduced in the 1920s and 1930s, a reduction from seven to two on a 6-car train was achieved.

AUTOMATIC DRIVING

By the early 1960s a number of people were looking at automating the driving function, one pioneer (surprising in view of subsequent stagnation) being the New York City Transit Authority with the Times Square shuttle. Dell proposed a scheme for London Transport following his established principle of separating safety and non-safety functions. The safety system was based on the well established coded track circuits, used for many years in North America on main lines for signalling and speed control purposes, and the Command or non-safety system depended on the use of audio frequency signals injected into short lengths of single running rail.

The proposal envisaged the automation of the driving function with a singie 'train operator' who could drive the train manually in case of failure, or on non-automatic sections. It was thought appropriate to give the operator control of the doors, partly to maintain his involvement. The Railway Inspectorate were fully involved and for a number of years would only consider one man operation on tube lines in the presence of automatic operation, which would drive the train to the next station if the operator became incapacitated.

One or two of us in the Chief Mechanical Engineer's Department (i.e., the Rolling Stock organisation) had also been thinking about Automatic Train Operation (ATO) and in particular the sort of braking control needed to achieve accurate station stops without loss of time. Our solution was to use mercury U-tubes set at different angles to control three rates of braking which could be selected by speed comparison at various stages during braking.[14] This rather amazingly fitted in exactly with Dell's concept.

When Dell set up a meeting with my boss Robert Arthurton (father of Ian Arthurton, lately LT's Passenger Services Manager) to set out his automatic driving proposals, I was invited to sit in. Dell's proposals for control of braking rates were a bit undeveloped and my suggestion of using mercury switches was accepted. Further, I was appointed the Chief Mechanical Engineer's man to take charge of our side of the project and liaise with Dell and his staff. This was quite a challenge as my knowledge of control technology was very limited - I had a rough idea of what could be done with relays but knew nothing at all about electronics.

I did not even know what safety principles were applied to train motoring control for example. I was vaguely aware of a 'two-wire start' technique, but when I asked for advice on how this would work with automatic driving I got no help at all. This was good for my personal development as an engineer, as I had to go and think it out for myself. Incidentally the question of what is acceptable when electronics are involved is still a live topic.

DISTRICT LINE TRIALS

The first trials of the system took place on a 2-car 'R' stock unit (these trains then had a 4-car West end unit to which were coupled one or two East end 2-car units, to make 6 or 8 car trains) on the test tracks available in the off-peak period between Northfields and Acton Town. The signalling equipment was provided by Westinghouse, including the train-borne Safety equipment and command translation

---

[14] Mercury switch retardation controllers have been used on London Transport rolling stock from the mid-1930s up to 1972. They consist of a circular or part-circular glass tube containing a quantity of mercury, mounted so that the mercury will move from the centre of the tube during acceleration or braking. Electrical contacts are provided to set a top limit to the brake rate (on the older stocks) or to control it between upper and lower values (as on the Victoria Line).

THE LIFE AND WORK OF ROBERT DELL

equipment. The 'Mechanicals' provided the mercury switch brake controls and a number of logic and amplifying relays.

Dell believed that any properly designed system should not fail, and invited all the top brass to view the first trial. As any other engineer would have predicted, this caused considerable embarrassment, principally to us rude mechanicals in that the first attempt at starting produced nothing at all. We identified and corrected a wrong connection and the driver tried again. This time the train started, but went backwards! My excuse for perpetrating such a fundamental error is as follows: Directional control on rolling stock is traditionally by energising No.4 train wire for Forward Operation and No.5 for Reverse. Clearly on a double ended train No.4 becomes No.5 at some point. We weren't quite sure where the change took place but assumed that it might be at the rear of the first car or 2-car unit. The connection box in the cab back wall should therefore be a good location to pick up the Forward wire. Alas we were wrong.

The third attempt produced a start in the right direction, and we accelerated along the test track. When we reached the point where braking should start, there was a fluttering of relays and we stopped motoring, but there was no brake application. The solution to this was not so easy to find, and it was several weeks before we were able to achieve proper braking control.

This was our introduction to what now would be called Electro-Magnetic Compatibility (EMC) problems. Switching the highly inductive contactors, valves and relays on the 50V d.c. control system could produce 'spikes' on that system of up to 1500 volts, and would almost certainly trip any electronic stick circuit - which is what happened. A programme of spike suppression had to take place before we could take the testing forward.

Eventually we got the braking phase to work and were in the process of refining that control when we heard that authority had been given for the construction of the Victoria Line. Further, the Managing Director, Railways, Anthony Bull, had approved Dell's proposal that Automatic Driving should be used on the new line. The development work thus had to proceed much more urgently so that a proven system could be ordered in good time.[15]

PRINCIPLES OF SAFETY SYSTEM

At this stage perhaps I should give a few more details of the system Robert Dell proposed to use. The Safety System used coded track circuits as used on the Pennsylvania Railroad for continuous cab signalling and made by the Union Switch and Signal Co, whom Westinghouse of Chippenham had a manufacturing agreement. Dell believed that with suitably selected frequencies, coded track circuits would provide even greater safety in train detection than LT's existing equipment. They also allowed signals to be picked up by antennae on the train as long as these were in front of the leading axle.

Dell decided on a carrier frequency of 125Hz to avoid the harmonics of industrial (50Hz) frequency, and used some of the traditional American code rates - 120 pulses per minute for track circuiting only purposes, 180ppm and 270ppm for restricted speed. This was set at 25mph maximum as this speed gives optimum headway on station approaches. For full speed Dell introduced a new frequency - 420ppm - which was to be electronically generated. All the others were controlled by pendulums and the principle of rising frequency permitting increased speed reflected the fact that the pendulum system was highly unlikely to drift upwards in speed (see figure 7).

---

[15] Robert Dell clearly had the Victoria Line in mind when setting up the early ATO experiments, but they were not described as being directed to this end. This may have been because of funding problems in advance of authorisation, or because he anticipated opposition within LT and hoped to persuade Anthony Bull, using the success of the early trials in his argument.

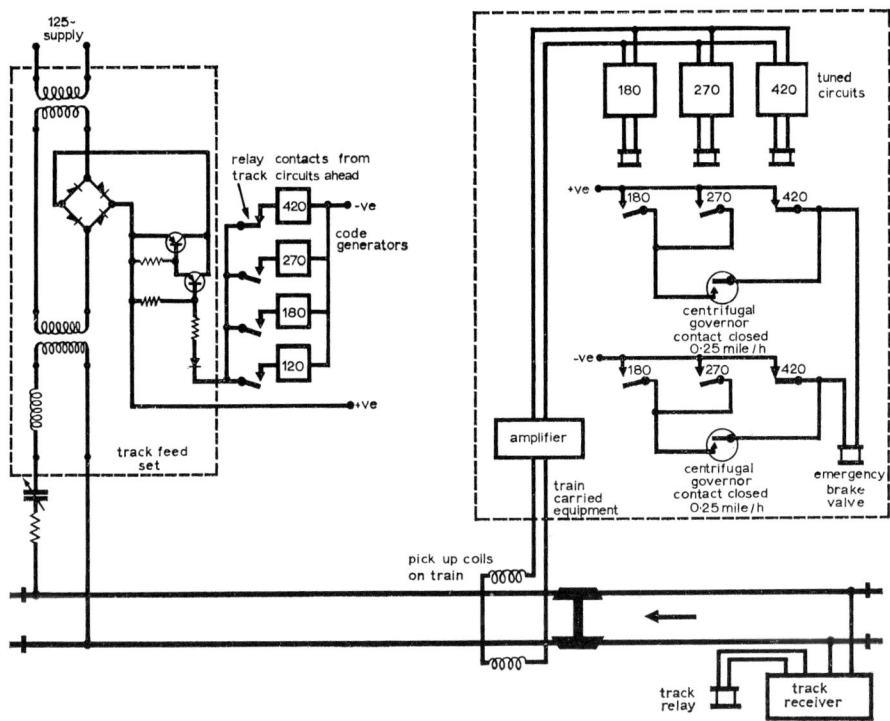

Figure 7: Arrangement of coded track circuit and pick-up coils of safety signalling circuit. *Diagram: Institution of Mechanical Engineers*

A crack in, or weakening of, the metal blade that formed the 'string' of the pendulum would cause its frequency to drop. If some or all of the bob weight were to fall off, then with this form of construction the frequency would increase. The bob weight was in fact in two parts, one of which was used to receive the magnetic pulse which kept the pendulum swinging. The other was used to pick off the signal to control the pulse rate. If either fell off therefore, no output would be produced.

The 420ppm code could be produced electronically because a downward drift could only give a lower speed signal and an upward drift, even if recognised, could only continue to permit maximum speed.

As part of the total train speed control package the Pennsylvania Railroad used a mechanical centrifugal type of governor which opened various sets of electrical contacts as speed increased. These would be used in conjunction with the code relays to seal or vent the brake pipe by means of an electro-pneumatic valve and thus apply a safety brake when a non-permitted condition was detected.

PRINCIPLES OF NON-SAFETY SYSTEM

As the name suggests there was no requirement for the non-safety or 'command' system to be fail-safe as the safety back-up was provided by the Safety System. What was important was that it should be reliable. It was based on the use of audio frequency currents being injected into a 10 feet (3 metre) length of one running rail. A second set of pick-up coils (see figure 8) had to be provided to pick up the signal as the frequency was so different from the safety system carrier. Signals of 15kHz and 20kHz were used to switch off motoring power and to initiate service braking for a signal stop respectively.

Station braking called for some accuracy in the stopping point (say ± 1 metre) without losing time e.g. by braking early to low speed, with a final stop from this low and predictable speed. The solution was to install a series of command 'spots' on a station approach with frequencies proportional to the ideal speed at that point. An axle driven tacho-generator (actually on the traction motor end) gave a frequency of 1kHz at 10mph and proportional to the train speed. Unlike the 15kHz and 20kHz signals the station spots gave a burst of 128 cycles followed by an equal off period, and when the train received a suitable signal it started counting both the track signal and that from the train tacho-generator (see figure 9). It is typical of Dell that he always insisted that these count values were 127 cycles, on the basis that the binary series 1+2+4.........+64 = 127. Everybody else knew that the switching was actually controlled by the next binary stage, i.e. 128, but rarely attempted to challenge the great man on his quite permissible idiosyncrasies. The 10 feet length allowed for 2 or 3 complete 128 counts so that if interference caused a miscount there were further chances of successful comparison.

Initially the station braking frequencies were set at 5mph increments from 50mph to 10mph.

Figure 8: A close-up of pick-up coils. The non-safety coil is in front and the safety coil behind. *Photo: London Transport Museum (LTB64/1221)*

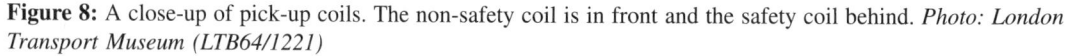

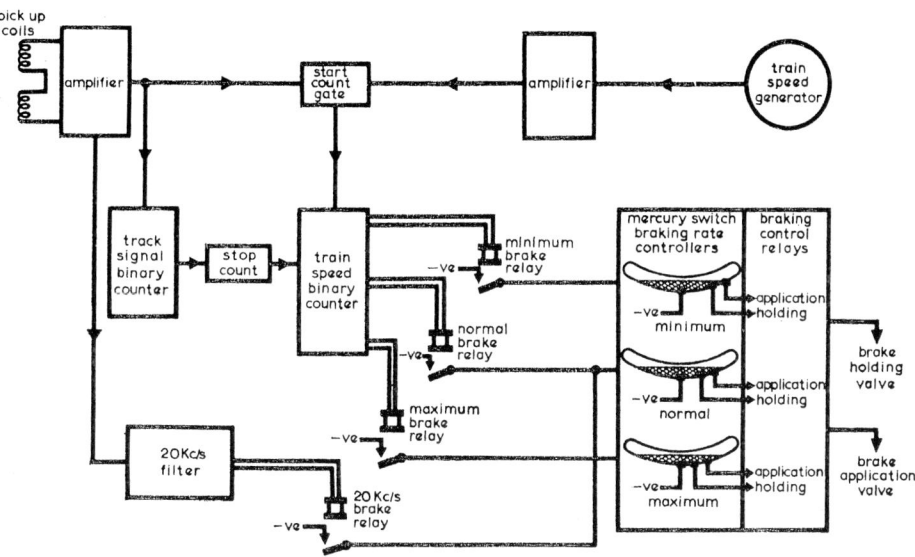

Figure 9: Command receiving equipment. *Diagram: Institution of Mechanical Engineers*

Later the intervals at lower speeds were reduced. Counts of over 136 caused the maximum (MAX) brake rate to be selected, 120-136 the normal (NOR) Rate and 104-120 the minimum (MIN) rate. Later a LOW MIN rate was introduced to avoid the tendency for a train to stay in the MIN rate throughout a stop. This used the pressure switch control of brake which had been provided to give a parking brake whilst stationary.[16]

The other element of the command system was the non-safety governor whose main task was to control the train's speed as nearly as possible to 25mph. It used the same tacho-generator as the station braking system.

This then was the proposed system but not all elements were being tested on the early 'R' Stock trial - in particular the Safety System was fairly rudimentary. The programme of pre-Victoria Line testing therefore called for:

a) a passenger service trial on the District Line with an amplified version of what was being tested on the test track, and
b) a more comprehensive trial installation on the Hainault-Woodford line with a full system which could be a genuine prototype for the production Victoria Line equipment.

Timescales for both stages were extremely tight - the Hainault-Woodford equipment had to be defined, ordered, designed and manufactured in 12 months. The District Line timescale was even

---

[16] Mercury switches can only be used to control brake forces whilst the train is moving - when it is stationery the brake rate is zero and the system calls for more and more brake cylinder pressure to try to reach a positive brake rate. An alternative form of control had thus to be provided to give a holding brake in stations, and this was achieved by the use of pressure switches which caused air to be released above about 15psi and pressure to be increased if it fell substantially below this. This sub-system is cut in when speed falls to below 4mph and gives an ease-out of braking as the train comes to rest, avoiding a final jerk.

shorter although much of the equipment was existing.

One element which was on order but not delivered was the mechanical governor (see figure 10). There was quite a problem in finding somewhere to mount this. Fortunately, in those days the 'R' Stock did not have shoebeams so the traditional American mounting position - on the axlebox - was available. There was just room within the loading gauge.

On the initial trial car the 'signalling' equipment was mounted in a big black box which was designed to be capable of mounting on a vehicle underframe. The only snag was that if any alterations were needed the whole box had to be lowered. As mentioned before, Robert Dell did not accept that changes would be necessary. The CME equipment consisted of a large rack of logic relays and the electronic governor. These were re-designed to fit underneath seats.

The equipment was transferred from car 22681 when the initial trials were completed to car 22682, which spent the intervening week or two in Acton Works being prepared. The actual fitting of the equipment and testing was done over a week-end. The train with car 22682 at its east end was put on a special turn which shuttled between Ealing Broadway and Mansion House. The ATO section was from Stamford Brook to Ravenscourt Park, being equipped with the appropriate trackside equipment. The driver switched to automatic operation before restarting from Stamford Brook and back to manual

Figure 10: The mechanical governor on the trailer car bogie, partially dismantled to show the contact arrangement, gear drive and suspension, taken on 25 March 1964. *Photo: London Transport Museum (3200/2)*

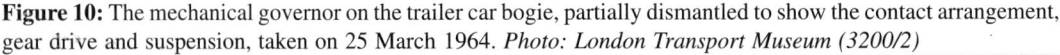

operation on arrival at Ravenscourt Park. (As only a limited amount of trackside equipment was immediately available only one station to station section could be equipped with coded track circuits and command spots. The most convenient section, with no junctions or other complications was Stamford Brook to Ravenscourt Park.)

HAINAULT-WOODFORD TRIALS

The District Line trials went reasonably well, and whilst they were proceeding work started on the Hainault-Woodford project. This involved preparatory wiring for trackside equipment and on the trains, whilst Westinghouse produced the equipment for both. The line had been chosen because it was operated mainly as an isolated shuttle service, although other Central Line trains traversed it to and from Hainault Depot.

The trains running the shuttle service were 4-car 1960 Tube Stock trains, whose origins would justify a complete paper in themselves. They consisted of motor cars with a cab and all axles motored, at the ends of each unit, sandwiching two converted old trailer cars. Fortuitously this motor-trailer-trailer-motor (M-T-T-M) formation was what was planned for the Victoria Line trains.

A massive amount of re-wiring was needed on the trains, space being made under the seats for the safety equipment, logic relays, etc. These latter and the electronic governor were dealt with by the Signal Department, and they used Style Q 'miniature' safety relays which took up a bit of room. The mechanical governors were located on the trailer cars, requiring additional inter-car jumpers, and of course the pick-up coils and tacho-generators had to be accommodated.

The 'trip valve' which vented the brake pipe to apply the emergency brake had to be designed from scratch as Dell insisted on a drop-away voltage of about 20. Normally E.P. valves on the 50 volt system do not drop until the voltage has fallen to about 5.

During the period between the initiation of the Hainault-Woodford project and the Victoria Line being completed, I attended Robert Dell's monthly meeting with Westinghouse. This allowed me to observe his methods and in particular his relationship with his main supplier. There was no question of competition on any of the vital signalling components as he would not trust any other firm to do exactly what he wanted. Westinghouse knew that they would get the work, but this did not mean that their position was comfortable. Not only were they required to work to Robert Dell's exacting requirements, but they were expected to anticipate his views without him actually expressing them. An extreme example of this was the Victoria Line Safety Box where Dell refused to give detailed requirements in terms of supply voltage variations, ambient temperature, vibration, etc. His reasoning was that if he quoted figures Westinghouse would only aim to meet these, whereas he wanted them to do the best they possibly could. In this case the policy backfired as when the first box was tested it clearly failed to meet Robert Dell's minimum requirements. Significant redesign and re-testing was called for, which delayed delivery of production boxes (see figure 11).

This was interesting in that Dell had been critical of the Civil Engineer's timescale for building the Victoria Line. At one of H.G. Follenfant's regular Victoria Line Project meetings when he asked for comments on the previous minutes Dell's representative Colin Docwra said, 'I have been instructed to say that these minutes do not represent a true record of what I ought to have said'. When the laughter had subsided he explained that Mr Dell thought that 4 years was an excessive time to build a new tube line and Colin should have said so. In practice the critical path analysis showed the completion date going back month for month during the first year and it actually took 5 years. The late arrival of Safety Boxes did not therefore affect the opening date.

In his office Robert Dell kept a work bench - nicely made into an attractive piece of furniture -

Figure 11: Two equipment boxes in place under cross-seats in a Woodford-Hainault driving motor car, 25 March 1964. On the left is the safety signalling code equipment and on the right is the 'auto-driver' unit which carries out comparisons between train speed and the speed commanded from the track. There are also two smaller boxes under another seat. *Photo: London Transport Museum (3200/3)*

which he would open up when Westinghouse offered a new component. They knew it was preferable to have it rejected early on rather than when mounted in production equipment. Resistors and capacitors would be torn apart to see how they were constructed and in particular how the leads were connected. He would frequently show the construction was far from satisfactory. One of his many informed preferences was for rolled threads in brass terminals. As he said, 'It doesn't matter whether the thread is rolled or turned, but if you insist on rolled, the material has to be ductile and we find that these never break'.

Another requirement was that transistors must not be used in a circuit where a 'wrong side' failure could occur. The Safety Box used magnetic amplifiers[17] for logic and amplification functions.

Some other requirements might be less easy to understand today. He refused to use plugs and sockets on any safety equipment, preferring rubber 'flippers' with brass terminations moulded into them. His reason was that if there was poor contact between pin and socket it was buried within the unit and couldn't be checked. When he used 'miniature' safety relays he insisted that they be connected by multiple screw terminals, and always claimed that there were never any failures caused by poor connections with this arrangement. Some of us wondered whether any lineman would dare to report

---

[17] Magnetic Amplifiers use the characteristic of transformer-like cores to amplify or to switch circuits. With no transistors or valves involved, their failure modes are predictable and the possibility of a 'wrong side failure' can be eliminated.

such a fault. We in the CME's Department screwed up our courage and specified plug and socket connection for our train-borne equipment.

Incidentally, one of the regular attendees of the Westinghouse meeting was their Chief Mechanical Engineer - O.S. Nock. He was quite tickled to find another steam locomotive man in this (for those days) high-tech oriented meeting.

Returning to the Hainault-Woodford trials, getting the trains into passenger service was quite traumatic and there were times when we despaired of sorting out the troubles. However, it was done and even a few weeks later we were quite baffled as to what caused all the panic. By the time that the Victoria Line trains arrived, the 1960 Tube Stock trains were regarded as the totally reliable back-up which was needed when bringing brand new trains into service.

One problem thrown up on the Hainault-Woodford service which we were glad not to have to face on the Victoria Line was the 'leaves on rails' situation. Chigwell Inner Rail approach was through a tree-lined cutting and by autumn 1964 we were getting trains running through the station. The wheel-rail adhesion could be so low that wheels could be kept locked even with the pressure switch brake at the lowest rate available. Dell introduced a wet rail detector which could switch in a special spot to initiate a low rate of braking at an earlier point than normal. It was not very reliable and in any case the dampness of the rail-head was not the only factor. Not having to deal with this problem on the Victoria Line, we left it to a future investigation.

Figure 12: A 4-car 1960 Tube Stock unit ready to leave Hainault station; one of five units converted to automatic operation for service on the Woodford-Hainault branch of the Central Line. The driving motor cars were built new by Cravens of Sheffield in 1960, running with converted pre-1938 trailer cars. *Photo: The John Talbot Collection*

THE LIFE AND WORK OF ROBERT DELL

THE VICTORIA LINE

A number of detailed changes from the Hainault-Woodford gear were made for the Victoria Line equipment. The improved design of Safety Box has been mentioned. More drastic changes were made to the train-borne command equipment, the relay logic being replaced by electronic logic and combined with the electronic governor and the brake control circuitry to form the Auto Driver Box. Surprisingly Robert Dell agreed that this unit should be a CME's department responsibility, probably because he realised that his staff would have quite enough to do on trackside equipment.

The general principles remained the same, the 15kHz, 20kHz and station braking spots and the 420, 270 and 180 codes. Even for the 1960s the small number of codes and smaller number of controlled speeds were unusual. Dell's reasoning was that, a) he believed in keeping things as simple as possible, b) there was no real need for any controlled speeds other than the line maximum and the optimum headway speed, and c) other systems were designed to give cab signalling for manual drive, whereas the London system was not intended to do this.

On the whole, I think his approach was justified although the set up at Kings Cross Southbound leaves a lot to be desired. The long downhill approach from Highbury means that if the previous train has not cleared Kings Cross platform, braking down to 25mph starts very early. Even if the train ahead clears the station immediately the following train is locked into a 25mph approach, the slowness of which makes it more likely that subsequent trains will also get locked into a slow approach.

The interfaces between track and train in terms of frequency tolerance, amplitude, etc., were the same for the Victoria Line as for the Hainault-Woodford line. It was therefore possible to test the Victoria Line trains (1967 Tube Stock) on the latter line long before their own line was completed. In fact each 4-car unit ran in passenger service for a least a few days. This experience, which threw up relatively few problems, proved invaluable when test running on the Victoria Line started in the summer of 1968. The first section, Walthamstow to Highbury, was due to open in September and a few weeks were allocated to various phases of testing, to be followed by several weeks of trial running, i.e. a simulated passenger service.

The first element to be tested, rightly, was the Safety System. In the event it was pretty well the only element to be tested as it was September before it could be made to work properly. The problem was that emergency brake applications were occurring for no obvious reason, mainly between Seven Sisters and Walthamstow. This is in the Lea Valley area and it was noticeable that the tunnel was very damp - the water level was near the top of the ballast. We suggested to the Civil Engineers that the river was leaking in, but they denied it, saying that in the hot summer wet air caused condensation on the cold tunnel walls. Whatever the reason the cure suggested was to run a lot of trains and keep the air moving.

This was however difficult in the circumstances as when a train ran it was likely to experience an emergency brake. This in turn, because the running rails were wet and rusty, caused flatted wheels, with resultant noise. The good burghers of Walthamstow, unused to having trains running below their houses, were already complaining of the thumping, so just running more trains was not acceptable.

The mechanism causing the brake applications was not entirely clear. The current rails were also wet and rusty so there was a lot of arcing at the shoes, which we thought might be upsetting the code detection. Sure enough, when the front shoes were lifted the number of 'trips' reduced, but the leading motor car ceased to do any significant work. Meanwhile the Signal Engineers found that the track circuit currents were very 'dirty' - codes from various sources were leaking into rails, via the wet ballast and producing mixed codes. The Safety Boxes were of course designed to reject such unclear signals, hence giving an emergency brake application.

THE LIFE AND WORK OF ROBERT DELL

With only a month or so to passenger service drastic measures were called for. Three were in fact put into force - a) Two trains, with the trip valve isolated and in manual drive were set to run continuously back and forward over each line - 'one engine in steam', b) Industrial hot air blowers were installed at platform ends and in the cross passages, and c) Acton Works manufactured 15,000 insulating pads which were inserted under the chairs by the Permanent Way staff to minimise leakage currents. The efforts succeeded but there was virtually no time to test anything else.

One problem which deserved more investigation arose at Finsbury Park. The Victoria Line had taken over one of the erstwhile Northern City Line platforms and one of the Piccadilly Line platforms, the other two platforms being used to give cross-platform connection to the Piccadilly Line. Both of the original lines had, at Finsbury Park, used an exaggerated form of 'hump station'. Normally this consisted of a 1 in 60 up approach to a station, level in the platform and 1 in 30 down leaving the station. It had been used since the earliest tube lines to assist energy consumption and run times and to minimise depth and thus lift distances.

For some reason, probably to do with the circular stairs to the main-line platforms, at Finsbury Park symmetrical gradients had been used but taken well into the platforms. The Northern City used a 1 in 30 up and down, the Piccadilly 1 in 50.

The mercury switch method of brake control gives a braking rate correct (in terms of relationship to the adhesion limit) for any constant gradient. It measures the gradient under the leading car, and the configuration at Finsbury Park southbound was such that the leading car could be on 1 in 30 down, and thus calling for a low linear rate of braking, when the rear half of the train was on 1 in 30 up, and thus for a given brake cylinder pressure producing a high linear rate of braking.

What happened was that the train over-braked, a complete brake release was called for at the penultimate command spot, and reapplied at the last spot but too late to avoid an over-run. Incidentally a 'Release' at the last spot was not permitted for obvious reasons. The situation called for some clever mathematical analysis, but we hadn't time to do it, so we got the Signal Department technicians to move a few spots to where we thought these brake releases would be less likely to occur. It was no better, so we tried again. Eventually the signal chaps said, 'One more move and that's it'. The final position didn't seem much better than the original one, but it survived for 20 years until the station braking arrangement was altered.

Another feature which caused a few troubles was the run-back detector. Before the Victoria Line was built, there were three situations which London Transport signalling systems did not fully protect against. These were: 1) terminal station approaches (later to be highlighted by the Moorgate disaster); 2) starter signal overlaps (traditionally of nominal lengths); and 3) trains which, against the rules, reversed on a uni-directional line. Dell had catered for both the first two on the Victoria Line, but strangely did not show any interest in the last.

The CME's department decided that something should be done particularly as the Victoria Line trains would be one-man operated, and asked Westinghouse to devise something. They produced a wheel driven unit which incorporated a partial disc which was rotated half a revolution by magnetic drag. In the reverse direction it shielded a reed switch from the permanent magnet which normally held it closed. The reed switch when open broke the feed to trip the valve.

When a train reversed, the run-back detector at the new end would be in the wrong position, so Westinghouse provided a coil, fed from the trip valve set button, to pull the switch in. No problems occurred with this system on the Hainault-Woodford line, or during early Victoria Line testing. However, when passenger service between Walthamstow and Warren Street started, we got occasional reports of emergency brake applications on trains sitting in the northbound platform at Warren Street. A little investigation showed that these appeared to occur when the previous train, starting out of the southbound platform, traversed the crossover and ran onto the northbound line. We then realised that this section of line was fed from a substation to the south of the station, and that the train ahead would be drawing its acceleration current through the rails under the stationary train.

One turn of a coil carrying 2000-3000 amps was enough to trip the reed switch, when the conductors were close to the run back detector, so we made a break in the negative rails and ran the cable on the bottom of the suicide pit to connect across the gap. For some reason we believed that the Warren Street situation was unique, so once trains ran through to Victoria the problem would disappear. We were wrong - exactly the same set up occurred at Victoria. Is the break in the negative rail still there I wonder?

The inevitable teething problems were sorted out without too much difficulty apart from two or three which persisted. One was the recurrence of station over-runs, at the rate of three or four a week. This was frequent enough to be an irritant but not enough to justify a huge test programme, nor to make it easy to observe an incident. I was very embarrassed having complained at the lack of information from train operators, when I was in a cab when an over-run occurred and was able to add nothing to our sum of knowledge of the phenomenon. Brakes were released half-way down the platform and re-application was too late.

Eventually we realised that the output amplifiers in the auto-driver box were failing intermittently due to internal open circuits in the potted units. This was also the cause of what might have been a more serious problem. Three incidents occurred over a few months where trains over-ran red signals. If a train failed to respond to a 20kHz spot it would proceed at full speed but at a full braking distance from the danger point, e.g. a train sitting in the platform ahead, it would receive a change of code from 420 to 180 and trip. The fixed signal protecting the station would however be located roughly at a 25mph overlap distance from the platform, so the train would trip well before it passed the signal.

In these three incidents, the train operators all insisted that the train had not tripped by the time the signal was reached. If this had been true, the failure must have involved safety equipment, so the Signal Engineers were forced to set up major investigations into the equipment in the relay room. Nothing was ever found amiss, but when it was put to the operators that they might have been mistaken, they were very indignant. By the third incident they were muttering that there were major safety faults in the system and threatening various forms of 'action'. This was averted purely because no further incidents occurred for many months. It was fairly clear that the original failures were caused by auto-driver components, and the operators forgot about their allegations.

A third problem was associated with One Man Operation rather than ATO. The cabs have no side doors, and a droplight is provided to allow the train operator to view the platform whilst closing the doors. This is interlocked with the start and motoring circuits to avoid the risk of an over enthusiastic operator leaning his head out of the window for too long. The droplight is also locked up when the train is in motion, but can be opened slightly to assist ventilation. It was possible for the interlock to be opened when the droplight was down on its ventilation stop, in which case the train would not motor. A number of incidents occurred during the first year of operation where a train operator could not get a train moving either in auto or manual. This meant that the train behind had to be called up to push the failed train out to the depot. As the second train could not pick up code the movement had to be at the 10mph Slow Manual Speed, and the total delay usually amounted to about an hour. On one classic case the second train could not motor after coupling, but fortunately the leading operator got his working and pulled the rear train out.

In most of these cases the depot staff could find no faults to explain the loss of power, and it seems likely that a droplight had vibrated down and opened its interlock. This was not directly indicated to the train operator, and if it happened to the window he had not recently been using, he might not think of it.

In spite of these troubles, which were to be expected in an introduction as radical as this, train staff morale was generally high. This was partly because the train operator grade carried a pay increment and was open to senior staff. The job was congenial and visitors came from all round the world, so they were quite proud of their association with such an advanced development.

Dell's concept and the implementation of it have stood the test of time remarkably well. Most of the safety equipment is still in use, although the auto-driver has been replaced by a micro-processor based unit. I was and am very proud to have worked with him on the project.

Figure 13: As mentioned on page 13, LT was a national pioneer of the Depot Yard Control Tower (YCT). The 1963 plans for Northumberland Park Victoria Line Depot proposed a YCT on top of the electrical substation between the covered sidings car shed and the lifting shop tracks. However, by May 1965 construction of the YCT was well advanced on the west side of LT's tracks. This photograph shows it on 9 November 1965, looking south from the second platform of the lighting tower. Coincidentally this would have been roughly the view from the 1963 YCT site, had it been built there. The shunting signal and point blades just visible in BR's Up Goods line (behind the YCT) led to the BR-LT link line, termed by BR the Back Road, for the delivery of materials and later the Victoria Line trains. The single line to the tunnel ramp in the background makes a loop east of the foundations for two car washing plants; their tracks and a fourth (to make a loop west of the washers) have yet to be laid. The flood defences, of earth and concrete walls, are shown, as is the extension (of eight braced units) to Shelbourne Road footbridge. This is a rare view as the footbridge was again extended (to eleven units with a new intermediate support) by 1970 to span more new sidings to be built on the left of the photograph. After delays, control of the routeing of trains by the YCT was scheduled to be transferred to the Operating Department on 27 November 1967. *Photo: London Transport Museum (5041/R/6)*

THE LIFE AND WORK OF ROBERT DELL

ROBERT DELL'S PATENTS

by John Tilly

John Tilly is 47 years old and has been involved in railway signalling for 31 years since leaving school in 1968. Between 1968 and 1993 he was employed by London Transport's Signal Department as: an Indentured Apprentice (1968-72); Signal Technician (1972-79); Signal Installation Supervisor (1979-84); Signal Maintenance Supervisor (1984-90); Signal Incident Manager (1990-93). In April 1993 he left LT and joined the UK Commissioning Team on the Channel Tunnel. On completion of this role he joined Halcrow-Transmark (BR's former Consultancy company) and has worked on projects for various clients including Railtrack, Northern Ireland Railways, Manchester Metrolink, Stanstead Airport, Channel Tunnel Rail Link, London Underground, CSEE Transport, Malaysian State Railways and Indonesian State Railways. He is currently involved in the Euston remodelling project, the first stage of the WCML development. He is currently studying Rail Systems Engineering at Sheffield University, and is also actively involved in the Institution of Railway Signal Engineers as Hon. Membership Secretary and Hon. Proceedings Editor.

Having worked for London Transport's Signal Department from 1968 to 1993, I can say that the subject of my paper is directly relevant to the environment in which I worked for those 25 years. In that time, I rose from an Indentured Apprentice to Signal Incident Manager. Dell's patents and his work for LT have greatly influenced my own experience and learning over those years.

A few minutes walk from the London Transport Museum in Covent Garden brings you to Southampton Buildings, the home of the Patent Office, just off Chancery Lane. The Patent Office houses millions of British and other patents and is a fascinating place to visit, either for undertaking specific research or if you have a more general interest in inventions and engineering.

During his long career with London Transport, Robert Dell took out 26 patents. The initial 18 begin with component parts for railway signalling and go on to develop remote control systems. However, they include two for monitoring the passage of vehicles (buses in 1939 and trains in 1959) and one (in 1955) for signs to guide passengers. The final eight patents refer to systems for Automatic Fare Collection, which was introduced to London Transport railways in the latter half of the 1960s. Together the patents make a set for automation of a railway, not forgetting that the passenger is as important as the trains, including he or she entering the car park and leaving the station.

The title of my paper is possibly misleading. Dell's first patent was in his own name, the second in his name and that of the equipment supplier, and all the remainder jointly in his name and a transport undertaking, with individuals added occasionally, plus one ticketing company. As you are probably all aware, patents are granted to protect the invention from being copied. It also gives the inventor a right to license his invention to others and thus make money from licence fees. I believe it is unlikely that any of Dell's patents were commercially successful in this sense. The patents also give information relating to the inventor's address - this can be useful in historical terms to, for instance, follow the inventor around the country. I hope that the following descriptions will give a reasonable insight into Dell's patents (joint holders of the patent are mentioned in brackets after the date):

Patent No.199150 of 18 June 1923 - Apparatus for Controlling Railway Signals of the Electric Light Type.
Patent application dated 18 March 1922.
The only patent in Dell's name alone, he is shown as living in Granville Villa, Finchley Road, NW2. The patent goes on to state, '.... whereby the "Danger" Indication is Extinguished when the "Clear" Indication is Illuminated, without Breaking the Circuit to the Lamp giving the "Danger" Indication'.

The Flux Neutraliser (FN) signal (which manipulates a magnetic flux in a transformer) was already in existence for two aspect (Red and Green) signalling, for example throughout[18] the Central London Railway from its 1914 resignalling. Dell's patent was for modified and very ingenious methods of varying the flux through the transformer which give three improvements to the original design and allow two FN units to be combined to control a three-aspect (Red, Yellow, Green) colour light signal. FN was widely used.

Patent No.215535 of 15 May 1924 (*jointly with Leslie Hurst Peter and Westinghouse Brake and Saxby Signal Company Ltd.*) **- Improvements relating to Electric Signalling Apparatus for Railways and the like.**
Patent application dated 11 April 1923.
Captain Bernard Hartley Peter had gone from being the District Railway's Engineer to be General Manager and Chief Engineer (later Managing Director) of Westinghouse, whom Dell entrusted with work as described in the previous papers. Major L.H. Peter, his younger brother, was later Chief Electrical Engineer at Westinghouse. By this time Dell had moved to Caddington Avenue in Cricklewood. The patent's objective was to improve the signalman's indicating devices and prevent faults on them affecting the signal.

Patent No.366224 of 4 February 1932 (*jointly with London Electric Railway Company*) **- Improvements in or relating to Lenses and Lamps.**
Patent application dated 20 December 1930.
By 1932, Dell had moved to 51 Eton Avenue, Sudbury in Middlesex, and he had named his house 'Delslivere' (Dells Live Here). This patent relates very simply to being able to give the optimum beam of light from the signal head towards the oncoming train and driver. It has been, and still is extensively used throughout the world.

Patent No.371055 of 21 April 1932 (*jointly with LER Co and William Stephen Every*) **- Improvements in or relating to Apparatus for Indicating the Movement of Railway Trains or the like.**
Patent application dated 21 January 1931.
W.S. Every was the District Railway's Signal Engineer, mentioned earlier by John Talbot. This patent improved on the 1905 District integrated system of drum describers with mechanical studs.

In this invention the Signalman at the train's starting point would still need to operate plungers 'describing' the train's ultimate destination and stopping pattern. This, through relay circuitry would transmit the 'train description' down the line as a series of pulses, as far as the next transmission point (e.g., a station where another train could enter service in the same direction). At each station between transmission points a receiver would, through relay circuits, punch holes in a paper tape to store the train's description (based on a combination of the letters ABCDE). The holes in the tape allow pins to make contact as appropriate to the description and thus through further relay circuitry to light the appropriate destination sign on the platform and where necessary in the signal box. The first description received would be displayed immediately to the public. A second description would be transmitted on the departure of the second train from the starting point and that description would be stored on the paper tape. The receiver was able to store many descriptions, limited only by the length of paper tape! When the first train departed from an intermediate station the paper tape advanced so that the second description could be read and displayed.

---
[18] Reliable contemporary sources differ: two or three signals may have been non-FN.

They were known as Ribbon Storage Train Describers and were used on the Piccadilly, Bakerloo and Central Lines. The paper tape lasted for about a week and had to be changed regularly. Signal Technicians generally found these machines frustrating as they required a specific knack and concentration to correct faults relating to the paper tape and when re-papering the machines. These machines served the underground system very well until they were replaced with electronic describers in the early 1980s. For many years a section existed solely to deal with train describer faults. Dell obviously considered passenger information to be important, just as we do today. Incidentally this was one of the first pieces of signalling equipment I came across as an apprentice back in 1969!

Patent No.499894 of 31 January 1939 (*jointly with W.S. Every and the London Passenger Transport Board*) **- Apparatus for Recording the Passage of Vehicles.**
Patent application dated 13 August 1937.
Dell's address reverted to 51 Eton Avenue, Sudbury. The 'Delslivere' had been dropped! This patent shows that he had wider areas of interest, as Eric Eden mentioned in his introduction, and regularly put his mind to other problems outside his own railway expertise.

In this invention Dell shows the fitting of a transmitting coil on a bus could be used to record the passage of buses past a certain point on their routes. The coil on the bus was activated by using a buzzer mechanism which continuously passes an a.c. current through the coil on the bus. The frequency of the current can be altered by adjusting the buzzer's rate of operation. A second coil mounted above the roadway, or Dell suggests set into the roadway, has a current induced into the coil as the bus passes. This can then be used to record the passage of a bus, past a particular point at a particular time. Dell suggested that by using signals of different frequency on different bus routes and by providing tuned amplifiers in the circuit from the receiving coil, it would be possible to discriminate buses from various routes on the recording mechanism. This was a possible companion to the train recorders and 'see how they run' clocks used to inform senior management in its efforts to control the system. Some of this had pre-dated the era of Dell's influence, and is described in J P Thomas' ***Handling London's Underground Traffic***, published in 1928. Looking ahead, perhaps Dell was considering a 'bus description' or 'headway clock' system? (Ronald Post will contribute some progress on this system).[19]

Patent No.520284 of 19 April 1940 (*jointly with W.S. Every and the LPTB*) **- Improvements in Electromagnetic Relays for Use on Railway Signalling and the like.**
Patent application dated 14 October 1938.
This describes changes to safety signalling vane relays. It proposes a relay fitted with two independent vanes controlling two sets of contacts arranged in series. The vanes and contacts were designed to operate together. In addition the relay has a latching mechanism that was designed to latch either vane if it failed to operate simultaneously with its partner thus failing the circuitry, and therefore requiring the attention of a technician. The illustration in the patent is not clear on the action of the latching mechanism. This relay reached a prototype stage but does not appear to have come into general use. I have been unable to find anyone who recalls their use. Dell did mention them in papers to professional institutions. I suspect that the additional mechanical components within the relay would probably have made it less reliable.

---

[19] The authors are aware of a nucleus of bus, tram and trolleybus devices. W.H. Challis drew an intriguing Bus Despatch Machine (Signal Engineer's Drawing CS4517 of 20 May 1927) which Dell himself checked. Another device was an illuminating sign (replacing a bell) outside Enfield West (now Oakwood) station to advise waiting bus crews that an eastbound train was approaching. This was probably automated - operated by railway track circuits, as the local signal box could be un-manned. A similar Train Arrival Annunciator was at Cockfosters. A ruling principle of the UndergrounD was 'to assure the easy transfer of passengers from and to trains'.

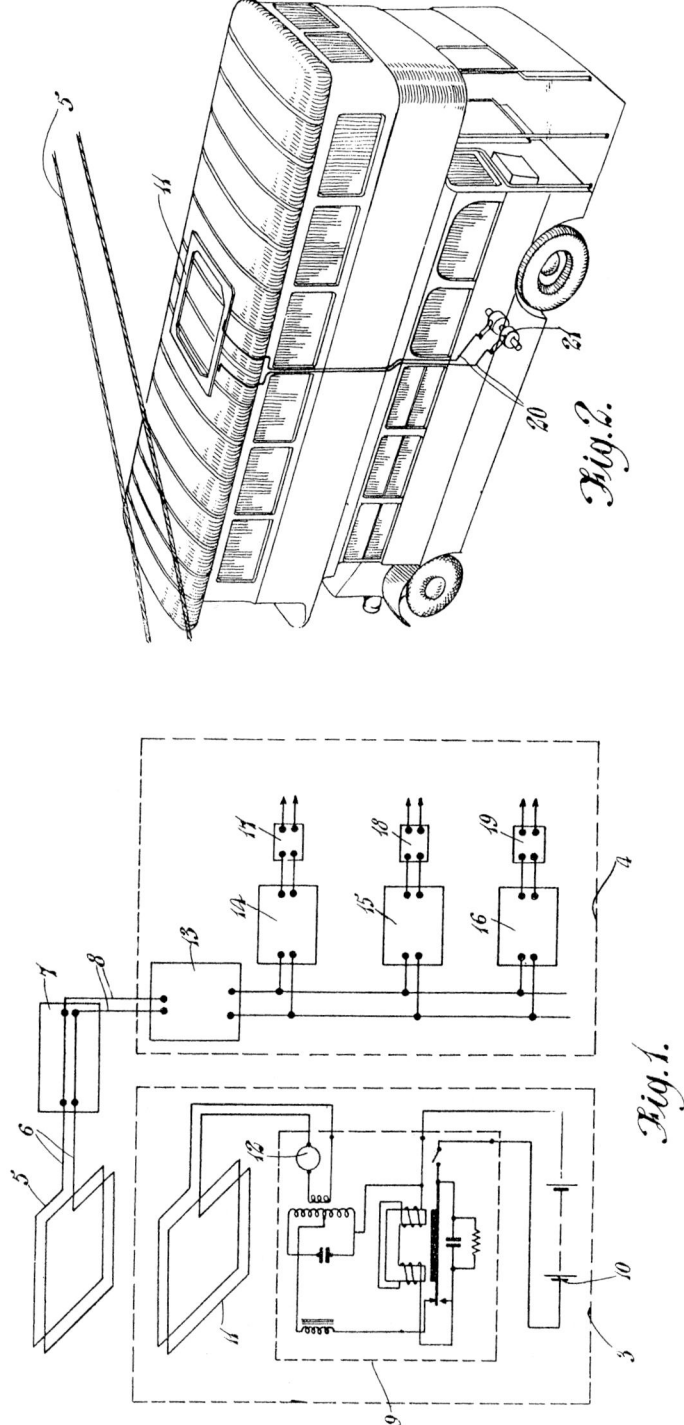

Figure 14: This diagram was submitted as part of the patent specification for 'Apparatus for Recording the Passage of Vehicles'. Figure 1 above shows on the left the buzzer mechanism which generates the AC signal in the transmitting coil on the roof of the bus. On the right are shown the tuned amplifiers that can discriminate between the different frequency signals picked up by the receiving coil slung across the roadway. The transmitting and receiving coils (11 and 5) shown in Figure 2 above are exactly the type which were used in the trial installation at Victoria bus station in 1938 to be described by Ronald Post. Only one bus route was involved in this trial so only one signal frequency was used. *Diagram: The Patent Office with the permission of the Controller of H.M. Stationery Office.*

THE LIFE AND WORK OF ROBERT DELL

Patent No.526824 of 26 September 1940 (*jointly with W.S. Every and the LPTB*) **- Improvements in and relating to Time Controlled Relays for Railway Signalling and the like.**
Patent application dated 24 March 1939.
This patent was for very successful relay improvements. These time element relays have been, and still are, in extensive use throughout the Underground system. When current is applied to the relay, the racked armature is attracted towards a geared mechanism which also starts rotating. The geared mechanism is driven by a small synchronous motor. The armature gradually rises and after the appropriate time delay makes contacts for signalling circuitry. The time delay is (factory) adjustable by a nut. When the current is removed from the relay, the racked armature falls away from the gearing mechanism, instantly breaking the made contacts and dropping back to its home position. Generally the signalling circuits employ a contact in these relays to prove they have disengaged.

Patent No.536609 of 21 May 1941 (*jointly with W.S. Every and the LPTB*) **- Improved Method of Operating Power Signalling for Railways and the like.**
Patent application dated 13 October 1939.
This was the opening shot in Dell's desire for automation of the signalling system, and with other developments, forms the basis of large parts of the Underground's signalling systems today. W.S. Every died on 12 April 1940, before the full patent specification was granted. This particular interlocking frame was installed at Shoreditch (see figure 15), as John Talbot has mentioned, initially without route-setting capability which the patent did include.

Patent No.629793 of 28 September 1949 (*jointly with the LPTB*) **- Improvements in Electric Cables.**
Patent application dated 1 December 1947.
This is one of Dell's simple and very effective inventions - encasing trackside cables in heavy rubber to protect them from damage. Such cables were, and still are, very widely used for signalling and traction current cables.

Patent No.652077 of 18 April 1951 (*jointly with the British Transport Commission*) **- Improvements in or relating to Indicating Devices Actuated by Impact or like Shocks.**
Patent application dated 6 December 1948.
This is another of Dell's simple and effective inventions - impact detectors for glass enclosed relays. These are designed to be dislodged if the relay is dropped, damaged or knocked, giving the technician a visible indication that the relay may have been damaged (the damage may be un-seen).

Patent No.725948 of 16 March 1955 (*jointly with the BTC*) **- Improvements in or relating to Illuminated Signs and the like.**
Patent application dated 28 January 1953.
This is another simple and widely used invention. For passengers who came only rarely, and wanted to make cross-London journeys between, say, Euston and Waterloo, the coloured illuminated signs (above passage entrances) saved delving into more complexities about different lines or routes. An example is preserved in the London Transport Museum. 'Follow the lights' was a sentiment voiced by many travelling families. The ruling principle of the 1930s further stated, 'In places where there are many streams, the following of a particular colour brings the passenger to the destination indicated without further reading of notices'.[20]

---

[20] 'Passenger Transfer Arrangements', Supplement to **The Railway Gazette**, November 1932, page 17.

THE LIFE AND WORK OF ROBERT DELL

Patent No. 748807 of 9 May 1956 (*jointly with the BTC*) **- Improvements in or relating to Signal Operating Systems Controlled by the Speed of Moving Vehicles, particularly Trains.**
Patent application dated 24 August 1953.
The invention comprises a short length of substitute non-magnetic conductor rail which is mounted on the opposite side of the track to the positive conductor rail, or according to the patent, within a section of the conductor rail. On a magnetic base plate, a series of magnets are mounted vertically with the

Figure 15: The first power worked lever 'Remote Control' signal cabin in the world at Shoreditch on the East London Line, with an engineer watching the system going through a final test. It is safeguarded in every way, in the event of a failure the signals automatically go to the 'danger' position. The levers move in response to master levers at Whitechapel (East London Line station cabin) half-a-mile away. *Photo: Popperfoto*

North & South pole faces alternating. Interspaced with the magnets are a number of coils wound around iron cores. The action of a passing conductor shoe generates an alternating current whose frequency is proportional to the train speed. This is then amplified, passed through a frequency filter and provided the frequency is within the correct range, operates a relay which can then be used to operate the appropriate signalling circuits. Widely used throughout the Underground system to prove the train speed is within a certain range, including deceleration and changing rates of deceleration, and for 'speed control signalling' schemes.

Figure 16: The 12-shaft style V frame being erected at the south end of Piccadilly Circus (Bakerloo Line) station on 23 February 1989. The curved pipes at bottom right (rear of the frame) are the air supplies to the motors. At the front of the frame are the mechanical interlocking (lower), handles for emergency working (middle), and electrical contacts (top). The frame was commissioned on 1-2 June 1991 and initially controlled from switches in the local signal cabin at the north end of the station. On 29-30 June 1991 remote control was transferred to a panel at Baker Street. This was one of the last of Robert Dell's remotely controlled frames to be built. The depth of the frame is 12 inches and the shelf 14 inches to accommodate particular documents. Ajar behind it is the rear of one of the well known 'submarine' doors used on LT. Their purposes included keeping moths from interrupting the photo-electrically read lamps in programme machines. The illuminated diagram has yet to be hung at one end of the frame. Frank Tuite began the construction of this frame, one of thirty-six he built.
Photo: John Talbot

THE LIFE AND WORK OF ROBERT DELL

Patent No.770187 of 20 March 1957 (*jointly with the BTC and Walter Owen*) **- Improvements in or relating to Power Operated Signal Control Systems for Railways and the Like.**
Patent application dated 26 April 1954.
Walter Owen, who was mentioned in Eric Eden's paper as being on Dell's staff, had joined the Underground Signal Engineer's Department in 1923 and was appointed a Senior Executive Assistant in 1950. He was President of the Institution of Railway Signal Engineers for the session 1960/61. The patent is for what John Talbot described in his paper as the power frame being straightened out from 'table' to 'upright', style V frame in Westinghouse's lettered series (see figure 16). Introduced in service in late 1954, and the most common type of interlocking machine on LT, it was one of Dell's mainstays in the drive for safe forms of automation. Part of the original machine, in passenger use from 18 December 1954 at Barbican, can be seen in the London Transport Museum.

Patent No.796062 of 4 June 1958 (*jointly with the BTC*) **- Improvements in or relating to Inductor Generators.**
Patent application dated 25 April 1955.
This patent is an improved version of No.748807 of 1956 and is basically a redesign of the train speed detector to minimise the effect of stray magnetic fields.

Patent No.809464 of 25 February 1959 (*jointly with the BTC*) **- Improvements in or relating to Apparatus for Recording the Passage of Vehicles.**
Patent application dated 14 March 1956.
I believe this is Dell's first full attempt at Positive Train Identification (PTI). The intention of this device is to produce a record of train number, time and train description at a given point on the railway. The train is identified by a unique number on its side. A trackside light and a scanner, consisting of ten photo-electric cells read the number by reflecting the light off the train number. This is amplified and then printed. Two other scanners print the time and train description. These are switched by a second light and photo-electric cell. The printing device operates by passing a current through chemically treated paper. The patent shows the printing head, a sample print and the train describer and time scanners which consist of rotating discs carrying raised imprints. Feelers detect the raised imprint and through relay contacts transfer the train description and time to the printing device. This is a case of a patent well preceding full use of the device. By 1962 train-side PTI was only recording station stop times at six Northern Line platforms (with signal supervision from one of the Leicester Square Control Rooms which predated Cobourg Street). The Victoria Line's 1968 'IDENTRA' PTI was roof-mounted, and the later Northern Line PTI is transmitted underneath the train.

Patent No.836625 of 9 June 1960 (*jointly with the BTC*) **- Improvements in or relating to the Automatic Control of Railway Traffic at Junctions.**
Patent application dated 2 April 1957.
The Programme Machine (see figure 17 and illustration on back cover) - Dell's third patent in his vision for an automated railway. Over 150 programme machines are still in service. Dell conclusively proved that these machines could be used for any type of railway scenario. He started by installing them at Kennington and Camden Town (the two most heavily used railway junctions on the Underground at the time) and followed it up by installing them at Watford, a terminal station with regular freight train movements and shunting, and Parsons Green, described in detail on pages 16/17, where the District Line regularly lengthened and shortened train formations for the rush hour services. The

Figure 17: The Programme Machine, patented between 1957 and 1960. Robert Dell is seated in this 1957 photograph. Behind him, holding the machine is Stanley Higgins, who did the design work (and later also became a joint patenter for valves in 1961). On the left is W.H. 'Uncle Tom' Challis, Dell's Indoor Assistant. *Photo: Alpha/Sport and General*

THE LIFE AND WORK OF ROBERT DELL

Northern and Victoria Lines are now almost entirely programme machine controlled, large areas of the District and Piccadilly Lines are also controlled by them, and there are a few machines elsewhere. Apart from the brief description given in John Talbot's paper, it is necessary to add that there were two types of machine: sequence machines scheduling the operation of points and the signals protecting them, stepped forward by the passage of trains, and time machines, stepped forward at half-minutes, checking the actual traffic against the timetable (both are shown on back cover).

Patent No.877150 of 13 September 1961 (*jointly with the BTC and Stanley Leonard Higgins*) - **Improvements in or relating to Electro-Magnetically Operated Valves for Controlling the Flow of Compressed Air.**
Patent application dated 23 February 1959.
Stanley Higgins (also seen in figure 17) worked at Westinghouse in Chippenham before joining Dell's staff where he headed the mechanical design team. This patent is for an electro-magnetic air valve used widely on lever frames. The advantages claimed by Dell are the absence of springs to assist in the operation of the valve. Air enters the valve from the top - if the valve is electrically energised air will flow to the motor via a connector - the exhaust port will be sealed. If the valve is not electrically energised the two armatures will fall by gravity allowing air to exhaust from the motor to outlet. The inlet port will be sealed by the armature falling by gravity and assisted by air pressure from the air supply. Widely used throughout the Underground, this patent is for a second generation component part of the V style interlocking machine described in patent 770187.

Patent No.980687 of 20 January 1965 (*jointly with the London Transport Board*) - **Automatic Electric Train Control System and Apparatus.**
Patent application dated 2 March 1961.
This was Dell's fourth patent in his quest for automation. In this long and complex patent Dell describes the control system for the Victoria Line. He explains the four command codes (420, 270, 180 or 120) applied to track circuits that the trains detect and convert into acceleration or braking commands and the braking spot commands that bring the trains to a stand at each station. Keith Ware has described this system from the train-borne point of view in his paper. This was Dell's last railway signalling patent. In addition to the train control system, Dell installed style V frames at all Victoria Line interlockings (see Patent No.770187 of 1957) and Programme Machines to control the whole line (see Patent No.836625 of 1960) thus giving London its first automated railway.

Patent No.982271 of 3 February 1965 (*jointly with the LTB*) - **Improvements in or relating to Apparatus for Controlling the Entry of Persons to, or Their Exit from, Enclosed Premises or Areas.**
Patent application dated 17 January 1963.
This is Dell's first patented invention connected with automatic fare collection. The mechanism is designed to allow a person access to or exit from enclosed premises and it is the forerunner of the ticket gates since widely installed on the Underground. The mechanism is released by a coin, token or other article such as a ticket, after it has been checked in some way. Dell comments that such checking takes time and not wishing to delay people proposes that the person pushes the barrier forward, and if the check is satisfactory a second latch allows the person in. If the check is unsatisfactory the person is 'ejected' into the adjacent area. The barriers rotate around the mechanism (see figure 18).

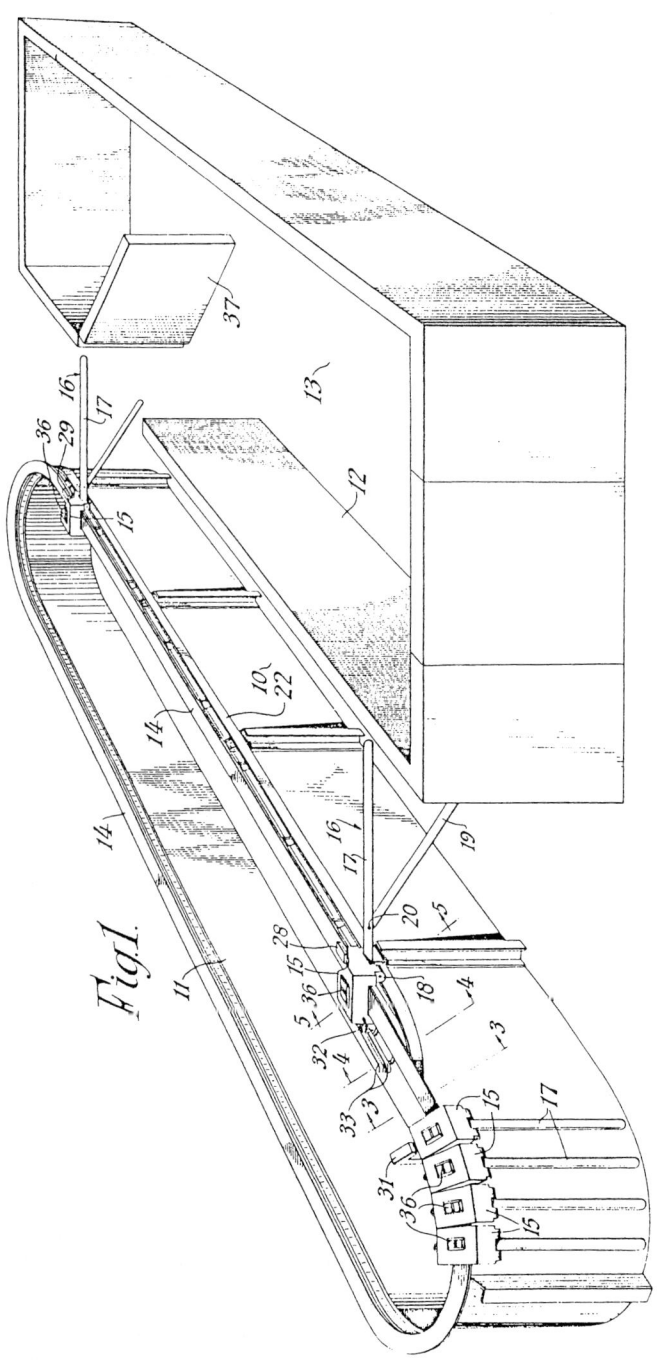

Figure 18: This diagram was figure 1 of patent specification 982271 of 1963-65. Upon the insertion of a coin, token or ticket in the sliding head carrying the collapsible barrier arm the barrier is released from the first latch position and can be pushed forward by the passenger until it reaches the second latch position. This provides time for the mechanism to check the validity of the coin, token or ticket without delay to the passenger. If travel is permitted the barrier passes the second latch position, the arm falls, the passenger proceeds to the platform and the sliding head engages with a continuously moving belt which carries it back to the stack at the entry point. An un-accepted passenger cannot pass the second latch position and is diverted into the apparent 'cattle-pen' on the right. *Diagram: The Patent Office, with the permission of the Controller of H.M. Stationery Office*

Patent No.1072690 of 21 June 1967 (*jointly with John Benjamin Crews of California and the LTB*) **- Improvements in or relating to Data Processing Systems and Apparatus therefor.**
Patent application dated 3 June 1964.
Dell describes a means of reading and interpreting binary coded data recorded on a railway ticket or similar medium. Once the data is read correctly from the ticket and compared with pre-set stored data it can be used to electronically open an appropriate barrier. The patent shows the coding marks on the back of a ticket. One of the additional claims in the patent was the ability to present the ticket to the mechanism in any direction. The binary coding could be printed normally, with impregnated 'magnetic' ink, luminescent or phosphorescent inks, or holes punched in the ticket. The coding is arranged in three groups each representing a nine digit binary number. This is used to determine origin, destination, value or other relevant information. There are also timing marks used to switch the electronic circuits so that the data is read correctly regardless of which direction the ticket was inserted into the barrier.

Patent No.1101978 of 7 February 1968 (*jointly with the LTB*) **- Improvements in or relating to Ternary Coded Ticket Reader.**
Patent application dated 16 June 1966.
Within this patent it is recorded that it is a modification or improvement to the previous one, the principle difference is the use of a ternary coding system. In this form the tickets have 6 groups of markings and a direction indicator mark. Each mark contains the following information:
  a). 7 digit ternary number - station of origin
  b). 7 digit ternary number - destination
  c). 3 digit ternary number - interchange stations
  d). 4 digit ternary number - shillings and route code
  e). 4 digit ternary number - pence and month of issue
  f). 4 digit ternary number - day of issue
The groups of data are produced on both edges of the ticket with the exception of the direction marking.

Patent No.1144254 of 5 March 1969 (*jointly with the LTB*) **- Improvements in and Relating to Means for Recording Data Magnetically on Record Media.**
Patent application dated 22 August 1966.
This patent is an important follow-on from the previous two and describes a device for recording the binary or ternary coding onto tickets at the time of issue in the form of magnetic stripes on the back of the ticket. The device uses a phonic toothed wheel, with each tooth corresponding to a magnetic marking on the ticket. The electronic circuitry is configured to mark the ticket as required, using small electro-magnetic heads similar to tape recording heads.

Patent No.1181842 of 18 February 1970 (*jointly with Advance Data Systems Ltd of London and the LTB*) **- Improvements in and relating to Record Media Transporting Apparatus.**
Patent application dated 8 June 1967.
This item is a mechanism placed within the barriers to read the ticket and let the holder through or not as the case may be. The ticket enters the gate (by passenger action) and is then gripped by a rotating drum and a continuous belt and driven round the lower half of the drum. A reading head reads the ticket (dependent upon which way up the ticket was put into the gate). If the ticket is to be returned to the passenger it leaves the barrier mechanism. If not, a solenoid operates and a flap closes to divert the path of the ticket into a bin. The reading head operates other circuitry to release the gate to the passenger. This was Robert Dell's 23rd patent, and it bridged into his retirement/consulting period mentioned in

THE LIFE AND WORK OF ROBERT DELL

Eric Eden's paper. Excepting the first two, all Dell's patents so far have given his address as 51 Eton Avenue, Sudbury, which he owned.

Patent No.1223121 of 24 February 1971 (*jointly with the LTB*) - Apparatus for imparting characteristics to tokens.
Patent application dated 2 June 1967.
Robert Dell's address changes to 1 Winterbrook, Wallingford, Oxfordshire, where John Talbot's paper mentions visiting him. The Dell family had this house since the 1920s: the working week could be spent at Sudbury and Wallingford was for week-ends (and ultimately retirement). The device patented was to magnetise car park tokens for use in automatic car park barrier mechanisms instead of cash (although the machines took cash as well). The unmagnetised token was fed into a chute and rotated through a powerful electro-magnet. The electro-magnet was switched on and off by the mechanical action of an arm and a spring loaded pawl. The arm also operated a counter for revenue purposes. Tokens were bagged into packs of 5 or 10 and sold at a discount to car park users over the normal cash payment.

Patent No.1223701 of 3 March 1971 (*jointly with the LTB*) - Improvements in and relating to token actuated mechanism.
Patent application dated 2 June 1967.
The Sudbury address is given. The device patented is the car park barrier mechanism - designed to operate the car park barrier with the use of a magnetised token produced from the previously described piece of equipment. The token is inserted by the car park user into a chute (it drops by gravity past two reed switches) and switches operate the barrier machinery and energise an electro-magnet. This releases the token in the chute by attracting an armature and allowing the token to fall through the electro-magnet - the token is subjected to an alternating magnetic field as it passes the electro-magnet which de-magnetises the token, making it useless for further use until it has been passed through the magnetising machine again. This is probably the first example of a re-useable ticket.

Patent No.1252731 of 10 November 1971 (*jointly with the LTB*) - Improvements in and relating to coin operated apparatus.
Patent application dated 26 July 1967.
The Sudbury address is still given as the house was not sold until 1972. The purpose of this piece of equipment is to gain a very accurate measurement of coins, both the thickness and diameter, and to check the milled edges of the coin. The combination of the three measurements can accurately determine the type of coin - pre-decimal e.g. 1/-, 2/-, 2/6d etc. The coin comes down a chute and sits on rollers where it is revolved. Another roller is activated and engages the coin to measure its diameter. A similar roller measures its thickness. The diameter is established by a light source shining on a series of photo-electric cells determined by the position of a mirror. The thickness is checked in a similar manner. A flexible arm reaches the coin's milled edge and as the coin rotates, vibrations cause an electrical signal to be generated via a transducer. This was Dell's last patent.

The question has been asked as to whether Dell initiated any more patent applications, which, (for whatever reasons) did not complete the process of being granted. I have searched indexes which do contain such material (for Dell's career period plus ten years before and afterwards), and I can confidently say he initiated no other applications with the patent authorities.

THE LIFE AND WORK OF ROBERT DELL

WRITTEN CONTRIBUTION[21] FROM RONALD J. POST CONTAINING FURTHER INFORMATION ON DEVELOPMENTS BY ROBERT DELL

Ronald J. Post entered a 4-year indentured apprenticeship in railway signal engineering with London Transport in October 1936. In October 1940 he was graded as Improver and six months later was successful in the power signal lineman examination, which marked the conclusion of his training period. He was then appointed as a Junior Technical Assistant in the office of the Signal Engineer at Earls Court. He did not return to railway service after the war and spent the rest of his working life applying the fail-safe principles of railway signalling to the medical use of ionising radiation, being employed by the Medical Research Council on their 2MeV Van de Graaf electrostatic generator and their three medical cyclotrons (Hammersmith, Edinburgh and Clatterbridge). He served on the Department of Health Radiotherapy Apparatus Safety Measures Panel (RASMP) throughout its existence. However, he retains an active interest in railway signalling and his membership of the Institution of Railway Signal Engineers.

John Tilly, in his chronological review of Robert Dell's patents, described Patent No.499894 of 1939 for a bus detection system, and displayed a diagram taken from the patent document, but he told the meeting that he did not know whether the system was brought into use.

I can confirm that the system was tested on one of the bus routes that terminated at the bus station in the forecourt of Victoria station (named Terminus Place on present day road maps). Buses working that route were fitted with transmitting aerials on their roof, fed by a signal generator installed under the staircase that led to the upper deck. A loop aerial similar to that illustrated in the patent document was slung across the roadway at the entrance to the bus station and the down lead from this receiving aerial was terminated at the input to an amplifier in the regulator's office on the north side of Terminus Place, with connections to recording apparatus at 55 Broadway. It was my duty during January and February 1938 to be at Victoria early each morning to take a signal strength measurement as each bus working the route passed under the aerial. If the reading was below an acceptable level, I had to replace the signal generator on the vehicle with a spare whilst the bus was on lay-over at the bus station. I regret that I cannot recall any further details of the trial, not even which bus route was involved! However, an article by S.J. Clark in **London Bus Magazine** No.40 (Spring 1982) refers to this experiment and includes two photographs of ST type buses working on route 44, fitted with transmitting aerials on their roofs and passing under the receiving aerial at Victoria.

I should like to take this opportunity to chronicle two war-time developments by Robert Dell, in which I was in a small way involved.

When night-time bombing raids on London by enemy aircraft became a regular occurrence, some concern was expressed that the arcing which can take place when traction current pick-up shoes leave the conductor rail at a current rail gap was 'breaking the blackout'. Robert Dell devised a scheme whereby a magnetic field (provided I think by permanent magnets) was set up at the point on the ramped end of the conductor rail where arcing could occur. The polarity and orientation of the magnetic field was arranged in such a way that the arc would be diverted into a chamber of insulating material installed below the conductor rail head so that the arc would be extinguished - a technology that had already been developed for use in high-power circuit breakers.

I remember assisting in a test demonstration for Robert Dell by pulling a collector shoe carrying a heavy current along a length of conductor rail and off a ramp which was fitted with such a magnetic arc-extinguishing device. If the polarity was correct the arc disappeared into the chamber; with the polarity reversed the arc was blown upwards with a spectacular flash. As far as I am aware this scheme

---

[21] Not read at the seminar.

was not developed to a stage at which it could be installed on a working track.

A second war-time development by Robert Dell that certainly was brought to fruition, was the River Thames Sound Detection scheme mentioned by Eric Eden in his paper. After the Munich agreement of 1938, steps were taken to guard against the almost complete flooding of the tube railway system that would have been the inevitable result of an enemy bomb penetrating one of the tube tunnels where they passed under the River Thames. Floodgates to seal the tunnels on each side of the river had been installed on the Bakerloo Line and on both the Charing Cross and the City branches of the Northern Line. These floodgates were closed when an air-raid warning was received and not re-opened until the all-clear had been sounded.

As the air raids developed, the enemy commenced to drop delayed action bombs in addition to the types that exploded on impact. It was realised that this posed an additional threat of flooding as a delayed action bomb in the river bed in proximity to a tube tunnel could explode and flood the system when the floodgates had been re-opened after the raid.

Robert Dell devised a scheme to detect the arrival of a delayed action bomb by sinking groups of four hydrophones on to the river bed at each of the points where London Transport tunnels passed below the river (near Hungerford Railway Bridge, London Bridge and Brunel's Thames Tunnel). These hydrophones were connected to the war-time engineering control centre. This was housed in the tube platform parallel with the westbound Piccadilly Line platform at South Kensington, originally constructed in 1903 and intended to form part of a proposed District Railway deep level express tube line to Mansion House, but used to house the Signal School from 1927 until 1939.[22] Space for the River

Figure 19: The Recording Room housing the River Thames Sound Detection apparatus on 29 May 1945. This view looking east shows the syphon pen-recorders in groups of four, behind them their associated amplifiers. Each group covered one site and a back-up spare group was also provided. *Photo: London Transport Museum (U36914)*

---

[22] There is a photograph of the signal school between pages 10/11 of **The Piccadilly Line - A Brief History**, by Charles E Lee.

THE LIFE AND WORK OF ROBERT DELL

Thames Sound Detection equipment was provided by the construction of a separate room at the west end of the tunnel on a mezzannine floor. Here the signal from each hydrophone was divided into two channels. One channel was connected via a straight amplifier to a syphon pen-recorder which produced a trace on a paper tape (see figure 19). The signal in the second channel went to an amplifier with a discriminating circuit which could detect the sharp wave-front resulting from a sudden impulse and cause the amplifier to give an output pulse. The steadily increasing sound from the engine or propeller of an approaching boat would not trigger the output pulse. The four pulses from a group of four hydrophones would release four needles above a rotating glass disc coated with graphite; the points of the needles would thus make a trace by removing the graphite (see figure 20). The angular difference between the starting points of any two traces was directly proportional to the difference between the distances of the source from the two hydrophones involved. As there were four difference values from any one site it was a straightforward matter to determine the position of impact. The system was regularly tested by firing a bullet into the Thames from a position on the Embankment; the impact of a small bullet resulted in a signal sufficient to release the needles onto the disc, so the arrival of a delayed-action bomb would certainly be recorded! There is a photograph of one of the hydrophones being removed from the River Thames on page 95 of *London Transport at War*, by Charles Graves.

Figure 20: The Recording Room looking westwards on 29 May 1945. Across the end are three groups, each of four amplifiers with two turntables inset in front. Each group received the signals from one of the three river crossing sites. To the left are standby amplifiers and turntables. The four needles above a disc were released by output pulses from the amplifiers when a sharp wave-front was detected by the hydrophones. *Photo: London Transport Museum (U36913)*

THE LIFE AND WORK OF ROBERT DELL

BIBLIOGRAPHY

PART ONE - Works by Robert Dell:

'Some Recent Developments in AC Track Circuits', **IRSE Proceedings**, 8 April 1925, pages 78-101.

'Power Worked Lever Remote Control Signalling System', **IRSE Proceedings**, 1942, pages 87-97.

'Developments in Railway Signalling on London Transport', paper read before the Measurements Section of the Institution of Electrical Engineers, **Journal of the IEE**, Vol 91, Part II, 1944, pages 400-418.

'The Maintenance Aspect of Signal Equipment, and its relation to Design', IRSE Inaugural Presidential Address, 16 March 1949, **IRSE Proceedings**, 1949, pages 28-36.

'Review of British Underground Railway Practice - Traction Supply', jointly with T.S. Pick, a paper read to a Convention on Electric Railway Traction at the Institution of Electrical Engineers, 20-23 March 1950, **Proceedings IEE** Vol.97, Part 1A (Electric Railway Traction), No.1, 1950, Proceedings at the Conference on Electric Railway Traction, pages 27-41 and 71-79 (Discussion).

'Control Desk Signalling Operation at Ealing Broadway', **The Railway Gazette**, 28 November 1952, pages 599-602.

'The Application of Electricity to Railway Signalling', Paper No.2301, **IEE Review**, April 1957, pages 165-172.

'Automatic Junction Working and Route Setting by Programme Machine', **IRSE Proceedings**, 23 October 1958, pages 85-116.

'Programme Machines on the Tube', **Journal of the IEE**, February 1959, pages 88-94.

'Further progress with the use of programme machines for the operation of automatic points, Underground Railways of London', **Bulletin: International Railway Congress Association** (English Edition), Vol.xxxviii No.6, June 1961, pages 395-404.

'Automatic Driving of Electric Trains', jointly with A.W. Manser, **Electronics & Power**, April 1964, pages 104-108.

'Automatic Driving of Passenger Trains on London Transport', jointly with A.W. Manser, Paper Number 6, read to a Convention on Automatic Railways at the Institution of Mechanical Engineers, **Proceedings of Convention on Automatic Railways**, 23-25 September 1964, pages 3-17.

'Methods of Control by Electronic means to increase the output of the lines and large stations (particularly Marshalling Yards). Utilisation of information concerning the line (characteristics and state of occupation) to operate the trains automatically', jointly with A.W. Manser, **Bulletin: International Railway Congress Association** (English Edition) Vol.xliii No.2, February 1966, pages 167-176.

'Presidential Address (Possible facilities for an automated railway - Progress of automated equipment by London Transport)', to the Institution of Railway Signal Engineers on 6 April 1966, **IRSE Proceedings**, 1966/7, pages 13-24.

'Fifty Years of Development and Progress of the Signalling of London Transport', Lecture Script, 8 October 1969 (*The John Talbot Collection*).

PART TWO - Other works:

Original historical records:

Ministry of Transport (and successors), Inspecting Officers' Reports, Public Record Office, Kew, class reference MT29 (piece numbers 82-104). *Note: A detailed listing of every Inspecting Officers' Report relating to the railway lines of London Transport and predecessors from 1862-1964 is available from Nebulous Books.*

LT Railways Traffic Circulars and Traffic Circular Supplements from 1934 to date. (A listing of these entitled **London Transport Railways Traffic Circular Supplements - A chronological listing from January 1934 to December 1991,** compiled by Peter Bancroft, has already been published by Nebulous Books.)

THE LIFE AND WORK OF ROBERT DELL

Books and booklets:
London "Underground" Extensions and Improvements, published as a supplement to *The Railway Gazette*, 18 November 1932, pages 15-56.
Improving London's Transport, published as a supplement to *The Railway Gazette*, 15 May 1946, pages 1-108.
The Jubilee of Automatic and Power Signalling on London Transport Lines, published by Westinghouse Brake & Signal Co. Ltd (c1955).
Fifty Years of Railway Signalling, by O.S. Nock (Institution of Railway Signal Engineers) 1962.
Route Control Systems, London Transport Practice, H. Firminger (edited by W. Owen) (IRSE) 1963 (and later edition by C.R. White in 1981).
Rapid Transit in London, published by Westinghouse Brake & Signal Co. Ltd (c1969).
The Story of the Victoria Line, by John R. Day (London Transport) 1969.
Underground Railways of the World, by O.S. Nock (Adam & Charles Black) 1973.
Railway Accident, Report on the Derailment that occurred on 7 September 1981 at Harrow North Junction, published by HMSO, 1985.
The Victoria Line - A Short History, by M.A.C. Horne (Douglas Rose) 1988.

Technical Papers (in addition to those mentioned on page 6):
'All-Electric Automatic Power Signalling on the Metropolitan Railway', by William Willox, a paper read to the Institution of Civil Engineers on 21 March 1922, **ICE Proceedings**, Session 1921-1922, Part II, Vol ccxiv, Paper No.4406, pages 55-81, and Plate 2 (Figs 1- 4).
'Automatic Train Operation on London Transport Railways', by W.W. Maxwell and D.K. Ware, a paper read to the Institution of Locomotive Engineers, 16 January 1967, **Journal of the Institution of Locomotive Engineers**, 1967, Paper No.686, pages 593-612.
'Speech Communication with Trains', by D.J. Norton and V. David, **IRSE Proceedings**, 8 March 1967, pages 197-227.

Magazine and Journal articles:
'Automatic Signalling on the Metropolitan District Railway', **Engineering**, 25 May 1906, pages 679-682; 1 June 1906, pages 718-722 and 728.
'Route Signalling at Rayners Lane', **Pennyfare**, February 1936, pages 55-56.
'District Line Route-Signalling', **Pennyfare**, January 1937, pages 7-9.
'Remote Control of Power Locking Frames on the London Underground', **The Railway Gazette**, 29 October 1943, pages 436-437.
'Maintenance & Overhaul of Signalling Relays', **The Railway Gazette**, 20 September 1946, pages 327-329.
'Improving Piccadilly Line Signalling', **The Railway Gazette**, 4 June 1948, pages 658-659.
'London Transport Power Signalling at Harrow', **The Railway Gazette**, 11 June 1948, pages 688-692.
'Camden Town Signalbox, London Transport', by Norman Crump, **Railway Magazine**, September 1952, pages 584-590 and 599.
'Last Electro-Pneumatic Semaphore, London Transport', **Railway Magazine**, March 1954, page 199.
'Remote Control Signalling at Aldersgate', **Engineering**, 27 May 1955, pages 677-678.
'New Signalling at Aldersgate', **The Railway Gazette**, 15 July 1955, pages 71-72.
'Speed Control Signalling on LT lines', **The Railway Gazette**, 12 August 1955, pages 189-190.
'Resignalling of Camden Town & Watford Junctions, LTE', **The Railway Gazette**, 9 December 1955, pages 678-681.
'Re-equipment of Cromwell Road Signalbox', **The Railway Gazette**, 9 August 1957, pages 160, 160A, and 161-162.
'New Signalling Device Leads the World - Machine that 'controls' the service', **London Transport Magazine**, December 1957, pages 2-5.
'Improved Automatic Junction Working LTE Northern Line', **The Railway Gazette**, 13 December 1957, page 690.

THE LIFE AND WORK OF ROBERT DELL

Magazine and Journal articles continued:

'Standardisation of Signal Aspects on LT', **The Railway Gazette**, 3 January 1958, pages 12-15.
'Resignalling of Watford Terminus, Metropolitan Line', **The Railway Gazette**, 12 December 1958, pages 711-713.
'Resignalling of LTE Bow to Upminster line', **The Railway Gazette**, 29 January 1960, pages 132-135.
'More LT Progress with Programme Machines', **Trains Illustrated**, December 1960, pages 756-758.
'Resignalling of LT lines at Barking', **The Railway Gazette**, 31 March 1961, pages 364-367.
'More Programme Machines for L.T. Northern Line', **Trains Illustrated**, October 1961, pages 624-625 and 629.
'Metropolitan Line Modernisation', by Charles E. Lee, **Railway Magazine**, July 1962, pages 445-453.
'First of its Kind in the World', an article on automatic ticket gates in **London Transport Magazine**, February 1964, pages 6-7.
'Another Important First For Our Railways', an article on automation of train services on the Hainault-Woodford line, **London Transport Magazine**, May 1964, pages 4-5.
'The Second Annual Members Dinner', **IRSE Proceedings**, 6 April 1966, pages 25-31 (contains speeches by Anthony Bull, Robert Dell and Col. D. McMullen, H.M. Chief Inspecting Officer of Railways).
'Trial Trains Running on New Tube as the Countdown Begins', an article about the Victoria Line in **London Transport Magazine**, September 1968, pages 2-3.
'Signals Staff Achieve Record Low in Vital Failure Rate', **London Transport Magazine**, February 1969, pages 8-9.
'March 7 - V Day for LT', by G.M. Kitchenside, **Railway World**, April 1969, pages 148-153 and 178.
'Things aren't what they used to be...', an article about Programme Machines in **London Transport Magazine**, August 1969, page 10.
'Fact Operation - LT Fully Automatically Controlled Train Development', **London Passenger Transport**, Number 8, July 1981, pages 459-462.
'BUSCO and the development of Bus Control and Communication Aids', by S.J. Clark, **London Bus Magazine**, No 40, Spring 1982, pages 27-35.
'Bakerloo Line Mechanical Interlocking Controls', by John Talbot, **Underground News**, October 1990, pages 364-367.
'Central Line Mechanical Interlocking Controls (West Ruislip & Ealing Broadway to Liverpool Street)', by John Talbot, **Underground News**, December 1990, pages 439-444.
'Mechanical Interlocking Controls Earl's Court - Bow Road', by John Talbot, **Underground News**, March 1991, pages 74-77.
'Mechanical Interlocking Controls - The East London Line', by John Talbot, **Underground News**, May 1991, pages 132 and 137-141.
'Mechanical Interlocking Controls Campbell Road Junction - Upminster', by John Talbot, **Underground News**, July 1991, pages 196-201.
'Central Line Mechanical Interlocking Controls (Liverpool Street - Hainault via Woodford and Newbury Park)', by John Talbot, **Underground News**, October 1991, pages 316-323.
'Central Line Mechanical Interlocking Controls (Buckhurst Hill - Ongar)', by John Talbot, **Underground News**, December 1991, pages 405-409.
'Signalling Interlocking Controls Bakerloo and Central Lines - An Update', by John Talbot, **Underground News**, March 1992, pages 100-103.
'Signalling Controls - Depot Yards', by John Talbot, **Underground News**, May 1992, pages 188-191.
'The Westinghouse Power Frames', by J Francis, **The Signalling Record**, July 1992, pages 102-111.
'Control & Interlocking of Tunnel Floodgates', by R.J. Post, **The Signalling Record**, September 1992, pages 131-135.
'Obituary - Robert Dell' and 'Robert Dell Bequest', **IRSE Proceedings**, 1992/3, page 10.
'An Accident & Its Aftermath', by R.J. Post, **The Signalling Record**, July/August 1995, pages 121-125.
'Experimental Point Heaters on LT', by R.J. Post, **The Signalling Record**, January/February 1996, pages 30-32.

THE LIFE AND WORK OF ROBERT DELL

'Can I please now have my five shillings', by R.J. Post, **The Signalling Record**, November/December 1996, pages 196-201.

'You don't argue with a Chief Signal Lineman', by R.J. Post, **The Signalling Record**, March/April 1997, pages 57-60; May/June 1997, pages 105 and 108.

'How a Signal wiring error led to changes in circuit design', by R.J. Post, **The Signalling Record**, *in press*.

Explanatory/background reading:

British Standard 376; Part 1: Railway Signalling Symbols - schematic symbols. First issued in 1930, Revised 1937, Revised again and extended 1951.

British Standard 376; Part 2: Wiring symbols and written circuits. First published January 1933, First Revision January 1954.

The Signal Box Directory 1987, The Signalling Study Group, Peter Kay, 1987 (see also *Amendment list 1* to this book, which was published in 1989).

The Signal Box Directory 1992, by Peter Kay/The Signalling Study Group, 1992 (see also undated amendment list which was published more recently).

Railway Track Diagrams 5 - England South and London Underground, published by the Quail Map Company, 1994.

The Signalling Atlas & Signal Box Directory, Peter Kay (published by the author), 1997 (see also *Correction List No.1* to this book, which was published in April 1998).

Figure 21: Cromwell Road temporary signal cabin in May 1957. This was one of the largest of the many temporary installations mentioned on page 16. It was in use, in a wooden hut, from 30-31 March until 20-21 July 1957. It enabled the lever frame in the adjacent 'permanent' cabin to be replaced by push-button desks, giving a net staff saving of five signalmen. The controls seen at the bottom are two or three position telephone type switches made by Muirhead. These were widely used for 'releasing' signalling (where an incorrect route was set or a train did not proceed after a route was set). They were used only infrequently for route setting, and seldom for a whole cabin. The layout will be familiar to present day travellers, with a few alterations. The new Triangle Sidings, right of centre, underneath the new West London Air Terminal, include No.31 which has been plated over on the diagram, as not yet provided outdoors. The solitary instrument behind the switches is a 'Winkler' for setting up train descriptions. The diagram is flanked by description receivers. The authors would like to conclude that although this book is about a great engineer, tribute is also due to all his staff, represented now by mention of the three who wired up this Cromwell Road Cabin - Chargehand Sid Lawrence, Pat Clarke and 'Lofty' Gillen. *Photo: London Transport Museum (440/227)*

THE LIFE AND WORK OF ROBERT DELL

EXTENDED CAPTIONS TO THE COVER PHOTOGRAPHS:

Front Cover Photograph (upper): An undated view of Whitechapel District Line signal cabin, code 'EN'. The Government Inspection report on this installation when new, was dated 21 February 1907. It was the last of the Metropolitan District Railway's complete resignalling of 'busy places' on which Robert Dell later trained (see pages 8-10). The code EN, also used on controlled signal-post number plates visible to drivers, was an American export - from the land where plains and mountains were too big to give geographical names to every telegraph station. Earls Court East was cabin EA, High Street Kensington EB, Cromwell Road EC, and so on geographically eastwards. Earls Court West was WA and a comparable series extended westwards. (The 'tubes' managed with single letter codes.) Although not shown in the photograph, the Whitechapel end of the MDR, together with a few places in the tubes, had, as far as is known, the first (very sparing) use of yellow as a signal arm or light colour. The front of the cabin is free-standing with a flat roof, the back of the cabin is sub-surface. *Photo: by kind permission of Wiltshire & Swindon Record Office/Westinghouse Signals Limited (K3653)*

Front Cover Photograph (lower): Interior of Whitechapel District Line signal cabin in November 1951. The signalman is working the 51 lever style B frame, No.85 of 1907, in the front of the cabin. In the back, a new 47 lever style N frame has been installed on rollers. For a week the signalman worked this while the old frame was dismantled. Overnight on 24-25 November the new frame was rolled into the front of the cabin. (An interesting rumour was that this frame was from No.198 which was originally ordered with 83 levers in 1938. This would have been for Edgware's new 1940 cabin, to control through running with Finchley and Bushey Heath. Accounts differ whether it was assembled or stored before being 'robbed' for Whitechapel. Certainly no new frame was ordered for Whitechapel.) The girder in the ceiling supports the panelled wall seen in the upper photograph, and the jack-arches carry the weight of the land above the back of the cabin. The cabin had to be ingeniously sited here to be mid-way between the furthest points controlled by it (the east end of the station and St. Mary's Junction respectively, seen on the diagram). *Photo: London Transport Museum (14629)*

Back Cover Photograph: As mentioned at the end of the preface on page 3, Robert Dell had a long and profound influence on LT signalling. Most of the equipment shown on the front cover could be replaced fifty years later by the interlocking and programme machines he developed, as described in this book. In his day engineers also directly controlled staff and held financial negotiations. A hidden irony of these three photographs is that Robert Dell deeply regretted negotiations failed to fund Programme Machines east of Tower Hill. This photograph of them is at Watford on 13 October 1958, a significant early installation mentioned on page 43. A Sequence Machine without a roll is above a Timing Machine without its cover. The vast changes made by Robert Dell's equipment currently safeguard annual passenger journeys of 866 million. *Photo: London Transport Museum (15383)*